MOU
BIKE

Mountain Bike Guide
Kent

by
Gary Tompsett

Published by The Ernest Press 1995
© Copyright Gary Tompsett

ISBN 0 948153 34 2

British Library Cataloguing-in-Publication Data has been registered
with the British Library at Wetherby and is available on request.

Typeset by EMS Phototypesetting, Berwick on Tweed
Printed by Colorcraft, Hong Kong

Disclaimer:
Whilst we have made every effort to achieve accuracy in the
production of material for use in this guide-book, the author,
publishers and copyright owners can take no responsibility for:
trespass, irresponsible riding, any loss or damage to persons or
property suffered as a result of the route descriptions or advice
offered in this book.

The inclusion of a route in this guide does not guarantee that the
path/track will remain a right of way; if conflict with landowners
occurs please be polite and leave by the shortest available route,
then check the situation with the relevant authority.

It is worthwhile, as a footnote to this disclaimer, to emphasise
that riders should give way to both pedestrians and horse riders,
and should make every effort to warn others of their presence.

CONTENTS

Route index map .... iv-v
Acknowledgements... 6
Introduction 7
Conservation and environment... 10
The Off Road Code 10
How to use this guide.. 17
Route text abbreviations.. 20
How to complete a route 20
Equipment and skills... 22
About Kent 27
Route Map Symbols 35

The routes
  1 Penshurst... 37
  2 Ide Hill 43
  3 Plaxtol 1.. 47
  4 Plaxtol 2.. 53
  5 Trosley 57
  6 Blue Bell Hill 1 63
  7 Blue Bell Hill 2 71
  8 Charing 1... 75
  9 Charing 2... 81
10 Wye... 85
11 Chilham... 91
12 Blean 1.. 95
13 Blean 2.. 101
14 Dover.. 105
15 Minnis... 113
16 Hythe 1 117
17 Hythe 2 125
18 Hamstreet.. 129
19 Lydd.. 133
20 Oxney.. 137
21 Bedgebury 141
Useful addresses 144

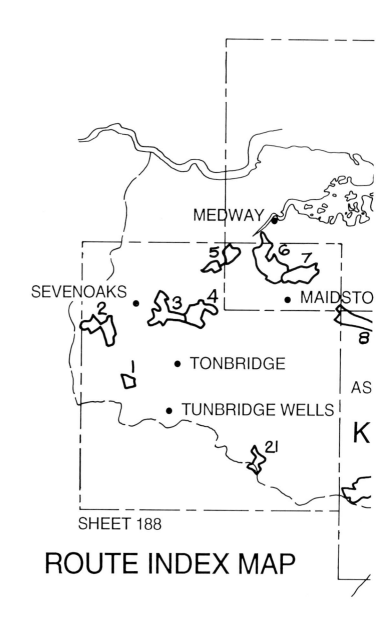

SHEET 188

ROUTE INDEX MAP

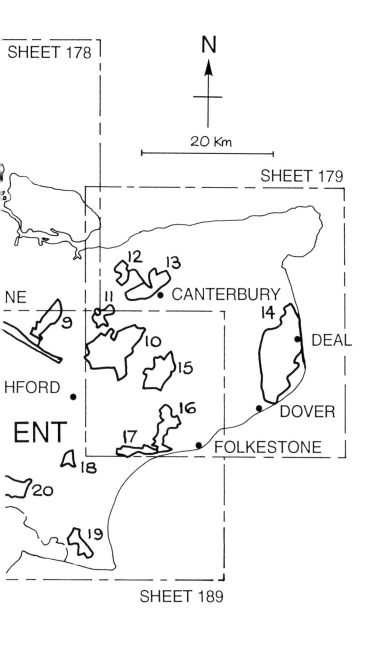

Acknowledgements:

Firstly, thanks to my parents, Anne and Malcolm, for letting me use their home as a base. It made writing a book on Kent, when living in Glasgow, that much more practical!

Also, thanks to my friends of the perpetual 'Recce Crew': Alan Thomas and Michelle Foster, Sas Matthews, Richard Judge, Pete Hahnefeld, Mark Gray and friends, Martin Bunyard, Charlie Holdsworth, John 'currant bun' Benardout, Anthony Cousins, Mike Stafford, Dad, Neil Wilkinson, Paul Lingham, Ken Jones, Jill Struthers, Ken Lowe and Aline Sinclair, without whom the book would be incomplete and rather self-indulgent. These people prove that mountain biking is the most unshakeable of life's bugs. They have also not been able to shake me off yet. Just think, if it weren't for me introducing most of you to mountain biking you would have saved thousands of pounds in cash and be leading exceedingly boring lives with no purple anodised bits. It's just not fair on their partners, widowed by mountain biking.

A general thanks to those people I have met who are putting so much back into the recreation of mountain biking and accordingly endeavouring to produce a nation of conscientious and competent riders; Jeremy Ashcroft, Derek Purdy, Colin Palmer, Paul Skilbeck, Paul Hinton, wee Dave Austin, Andy Stephenson, Rob Howard, Mike Westphal at PORC, Tony Wilsher at Larkfield Cycles, Roger Dillon and Andrew Denton of Polaris and Challenge Events, Graham Longstaff, Nicky Crowther and Andy Dickson of Mountain Biker International magazine and Tym Manley of MBUK.

Thank you, Naomi, for checking through the text, and drinking all my Scotch.

Good fortune enabled me to meet Susan Hodgkiss in Kent in 1991. Without this chance meeting, the idea for this book may never have materialised. I would therefore like to thank Susan and Peter Hodgkiss for the inspiration and opportunity. The publishers acknowledge editorial and production supervision by Susan Hodgkiss.

Lastly, thanks to the Kent County Council, who provide a superb level of public right of way maintenance and service.

INTRODUCTION

The words mountain biking and Kent seem mutually exclusive. This is not the case. Although a generally low lying county in a densely populated part of the country, Kent offers a varied and often exciting range of routes for the off road cyclist, with trails less frequented than many of those in supposedly remote areas elsewhere in the country. This car-bound county takes on a whole new form when you are within the often heavily wooded countryside. In the guide are 21 circular routes in this terrain, comprising a wide range of length and difficulty to suit everyone – from the family group to the faster solo rider. Distances vary from 5 to 50 kilometres, (3 to 30 miles).

The routes are spread around the county, on the Downs, Weald and marshes. The only area not covered, due to lack of available trails, is the triangular basin occupied by the rivers Medway and Beult. Delightful road routes could be explored here between Maidstone, Tonbridge and Tenterden.

The routes have different aims, and these are described in the introduction to each route. You will, of course, have different experiences, dependent on factors such as the weather, your fitness and health, and bike reliability. I cannot guarantee a religious experience or perfect weather with no mud, but I can say that you will have travelled on a legal, well-researched scenic route in 'the garden of England'. If you wish to pursue more advanced aspects of the sport, then there is an active racing scene with several clubs and venues operating on private land. There is even a route that incorporates the unique venue of Penshurst Off Road Club, a mountain biking centre that caters for all abilities. A discount is available for entry upon production of this guidebook. See 'Useful Addresses'.

Kent has a comparatively large network of public rights of way, containing 3.5% of the national network. 8,945km of road, 225km of BOATS and Green lanes, and 6,513km of bridleways and footpaths. (Adjacent south-east counties have about 40% less). This guide uses existing public rights of way as the basis for the routes.

Kent county has been the subject of recent feasibility studies in cycling. The Kent Recreational Cycling Study has been compiled by Sustrans – a registered charity specialising in the development and creation of dedicated cycling routes. They endeavour to use promenades, river valleys, canal towpaths, disused railways and forest roads, as well as existing rights of way. This also benefits walkers and horse-riders, with increased access, better surfaces, and exclusive waymarking. Their work is mentioned here (and at key points in the route text) in the hope that pressure from this charity and yourselves, the readers, will ultimately lead to improved facilities for off road cycling in the county.

Sustrans' view of Kent is encouraging. They can recognise an obvious market for cycling routes. 6% of visitors to Kent are cyclists, many of whom are from London and France, and today, more bicycles are sold than cars in Kent. Although Kent has a lot of traffic, they have been able to recommend a network of routes that are safe for families. Most of these would require careful negotiation to enable access prior to their commissioning and, therefore, it may be some time before they are up and running. Below is a list of the proposed Sustrans routes totalling some 800km, 200 of which are traffic free.

- Coastal route, Dartford to Dungeness.
- Canterbury network.
- Medway Valley, Penshurst to Chatham.
- Darent Valley to Sevenoaks and Sevenoaks network.
- Routes on minor roads.
- International termini routes; Dover, Sheerness, Ramsgate, Folkestone, Ashford International (Channel Tunnel), Lydd, and Gatwick Airport (Forest Way and Worth Way from Tunbridge Wells).

The county has a public rights of way strategy and transport policy that should put cyclists firmly on a safer routing. Their strategy includes aspects of Definition, Protection, Management, Maintenance, Development and Promotion. A particularly practical application of the maintenance aspect has been to recruit volunteers to help with the work. The Parish Paths Initiative and North Downs Way Volunteer Wardens are examples of this, and I would encourage you to get involved, as you will then be putting something back into the sport. At the very least, contact the KCC when you find a problem on a path – they will send you an action sheet to fill in (see Useful addresses).

An exciting addition to Kent's cycling portfolio is Le Tour, (Tour de France), with the route in 1994 passing through Dover, Folkestone, Canterbury, Ashford, the Weald and Tunbridge Wells before moving on to Sussex.

CONSERVATION AND THE ENVIRONMENT

However desperate you are to get out on your bike, please pause to read this section. Information contained here may save unnecessary and unfortunate incidents occurring on a ride.

Mountain bike access to the countryside is a sensitive issue and you represent the whole body of off road cycling when you are on the trails – so stick to public rights of way and travel with minimum impact. Ride in such a way that you leave no trace of your passing. Try not to skid, and when encountering puddles or mud, try to cycle through them and not around them, as this widens the path. Avoid tracks that could be eroded after rainfall.

There are many organisations you can join, to help with the maintenance of the countryside, and they nearly all depend on volunteers and fund-raising to survive. See 'Useful Addresses'.

THE OFF ROAD CODE

This code is published in many magazines and should be supplied with the purchase of all new mountain bikes. It is endorsed by the Countryside Commission and the Sports Council and includes information on access rights, safety, and the highway code:

- Only ride where you know you have a legal right.
- Always give way to horses and pedestrians.
- Avoid animals and crops.
- Take all litter with you.

- Leave all gates as found.
- Keep the noise down.
- Don't get annoyed with anyone, it never solves problems.
- Always try to be self-sufficient, for you and your bike.
- Never create a fire hazard.

It also insists that you abide by the Country Code as listed below.

- Enjoy the countryside and respect its life and work.
- Guard against the risk of fire.
- Fasten all gates.
- Keep your dogs under close control.
- Keep to rights of way across farmland.
- Use gates and stiles to cross fences, hedges and walls.
- Leave livestock, crops and machinery alone.
- Take your litter home.
- Help keep all water clean.
- Protect wildlife, plants and trees.
- Take special care on country roads.
- Make no unnecessary noise.

Impact

Mountain bikes themselves cause no conflict of use with other 'Non-Motorised Users' — it is the riders. You are responsible for the safety of yourself and all other NMUs. It is unlikely that any other users will be travelling as fast as you, and you must therefore give way, by law — so slow down. There is a lot to be said about trail manners, and I have seen some unfortunate incidents caused by mountain bikers, — don't let it be you. Please heed the cautionary tales below.

Horses: 'A cyclist slowly pulls up behind the group of horses, learner riders in mount. One horse hears a strange whirring sound, turns and sees a dash of colour. Alarmed, it careers off the trail into the woods. The rider is knocked off by a low branch.' I have also seen horse-riders' legs nearly shredded on barbed wire fences, when their horse has gone out of control. Horses need to be hailed. That is, start talking, from some distance, to the riders. The horse needs to know that you are a human and not a UFO. Stop, get off the bike and get right into the side when approaching horses. They are very unpredictable. Ask the rider whether the horse is OK with bikes. (No, I don't mean whether it can ride one). Horses are very common on Kent's highways.

Sheep: 'The cyclist continued down the narrow track with the sheep scattering in front of him. Several were running ahead for hundreds of metres, and the rider did not slow until he reached the gate. Exhausted, the lambing ewe's legs buckled under her.' Just think about it.

Dogs: Similarly, these run everywhere. Just make sure that you are not the cause. Even if they appear under control, slow down, talk to the owner and pass.

People: 'The family were unsure which way to scatter as the bikes came screaming down the bridleway in a popular country park. As the parents parted, the small child was left standing in the middle of the track, and the bikes passed on either side of her. The most mature of the group, Paul, a racer and ambassador for the sport, cycled down some minutes later, at a more sedate pace. He said to the rest of the group that he would not have gone at that speed and that they had been reckless. They still felt pleased to have beaten him. It was some while later before they realised the full extent of what Paul had said.' Although people are a little more predictable than four-legged animals, you still must slow right down, announce your presence with a greeting and a thank you before passing with care – particularly from behind as their hearing may not be too good.

Cyclists: 'Richard loved the smooth path through the woods, with its twists and turns, rises and falls. So did the other rider. They met head-on at 20 mph. Richard still rides, the scars have healed now.'

In Kent, you will meet other trail users, often in the most unexpected places, so ensure that you are travelling at such a speed that you will not come into conflict with these users. Precautions include: not riding faster than your visible stopping distance (blind turns), not wearing dark glasses in woodland and not going so fast over technical ground that you are unable to look ahead at least 50 metres.

In addition, if you can, time your ride to take place at a quieter time of the day. That is, in summer, try early morning and evening rides and always try and ride on a Saturday in preference to Sunday – it is much quieter on the trails then.

To lessen impact, ride in small groups (less than six). If you cannot avoid a large group, then split into smaller parties, leave at different times or choose different rotations or routes.

Access

The routes in this book use public rights of way, as defined on the county 1:10,000 scale definitive maps and their attached statements. You should be familiar with the Ordnance Survey symbols and classifications for public rights of way and the definitions and rights outlined below.

If anyone disputes your presence on a path, then explain your understanding of access rights to them, and use the map to show your position. Stay calm and courteous. If they still insist that you are not on a public right of way then apologise and ask for advice on the most appropriate direction in which to leave. Investigate the discrepancy at a later date. Since mistakes can be made and changes in the network do occur, the descriptions of routes in this book cannot be taken as proof of a right of way. Here are some current facts:

Trespass – This is when you are on someone else's land without their permission, unless you are passing and re-passing on a public right of way. You must not stop for too long, use illegitimate equipment or behave unreasonably.

Bridleways – Public have right of way on foot, pedal cycle and horse. Cyclists must give way to horses and pedestrians. Markings on the ground should be in blue.

Byways: Byway open to all traffic (BOAT) – Public have right of way on foot and most other forms of wheeled vehicle. Markings on the ground should be in red.

Footpaths – Cyclists have **no** right of way to ride on a footpath. Markings on the ground should be in yellow.

Road used as a public path (RUPP) – Public highway that has yet to have detailed classification. Their minimum status is usually that of bridleway, so that cyclists may use them.

However, this is not to say that if vehicles are allowed to use them, cyclists can as well. The county authorities are obliged to review the status of these highways. They were derived from the previous classifications of Carriage Road/Footpath (CRF) and Carriage Road/Bridleway (CRB) and are not always surfaced or marked on the ground.

White or Green lanes – These words have no legal meaning. White lanes are so called as they are shown as white on the Ordnance Survey 1:50,000 and are often surfaced, whereas Green lanes although shown similarly in white are often unsurfaced and grassy in appearance. These highways may be public or private.

Unclassified County Roads (UCRs) – Most, if not all are open to the public, and are shown on the Ordnance Survey 1:50,000 in yellow, often terminating in dead-ends, or leading to other public rights of way. These roads are listed as maintainable highways in county records.

Permissive paths – These paths are established by local landowners for the explicit use of certain users. The public have no right, just the owner's permission to pass along them. I do not know of any for cyclists. They will be marked on the ground in many ways. Those marked as permissive bridleways should only be used by horse-riders.

Toll rides – These are paths established by the landowner for the explicit use of horse-riders only.

Canal towpaths – These can be privately owned, subject to local bylaws, or owned by British Waterways. This authority requires a cycling permit to be purchased for a small fee. However, they have no property in Kent.

Pavements – Cycling is not permitted on pavements.

Designated cycle paths – These can be in towns, parks or forests, but there are few in Kent. Look out for exclusive cycling signs.

Bylaws – These may be enforced locally, and when displayed, must be observed.

Traffic Regulation Orders (TROs) – These may also be enforced locally, and when displayed, must be observed.

Long distance paths – These carry no extra rights, and are not predominantly footpaths. Kent has several long distance paths – the North Downs Way at 227km, the Wealdway at 130km, the Saxon Shore Way at 227km (which follows the old Saxon shoreline connecting the old Roman forts of Reculver, Richborough, Lemanis at Lympne and Anderida at Pevensey), the Greensand Way at 150km and a few ancient ways, such as the trackway along the top of the Downs and the Pilgrims Way along the bottom.

It is also not normal to have access to the following areas on a bicycle: picnic sites, country parks, open country, open spaces, National Trust property, English Nature property, environmentally sensitive areas (ESAs), areas of outstanding natural beauty (AONB), sites of special scientific interest (SSSI), common land, heaths, village greens (locals only), beaches (dunes and foreshore), nature reserves, parks and grounds of stately homes and castles, lakes, rivers and canals. You may not even be able to cycle in the carparks of these amenities. By now you must be itching to ride the legal routes in this book!

The Forestry Commission (Land managed by The Forestry Enterprise) – Cycling is encouraged in most of their forests through an open access policy. Their tracks are particularly suitable for beginners and family groups. The Ordnance Survey map should not be used to define the boundary of the land owned by the Commission. Instead, local information should be sought. The forests are working environments and therefore there are times when tracks are closed. At these times notices should be strictly observed in the interests of your own safety. An issue currently receiving much media coverage is the gradual sale of Forestry Commission land and the subsequent loss of public access. I would advise that you still set out to follow routes on Forestry Commission land, but check the latest local situation once you are there.

Races – It is illegal to promote or take part in races on public rights of way.

HOW TO USE THIS GUIDE

Route selection
An index to all routes is provided firstly as a 'Route Index Map', and secondly as a 'Route Summary Chart'. By referring to these you may select a route according to its location, length or grade. Also, these indexes can be used to see possible route combinations. General information is given at the start of all route descriptions on places of interest that are on, or close to, the route.

Route grading

Routes are graded according to a combination of the following factors: distance, usual ground conditions, technical sections, navigational complexity and ascent. The grades are:

Easy – suitable for fit family groups and children.
Moderate – suitable for teenagers, adults and regular riders.
Difficult – suitable for more experienced riders and optimists.

Route timing

Times for a route can only be established by the rider. They are variable, and dependent on a number of factors, unlike distance, which is a constant. Therefore the times given are based on those of an average rider, at an average pace, in fair weather and including a half-hour stop for lunch. After you have done a few of the rides you should make a note of your average speed and use this to estimate your time for subsequent routes. 10 kilometres per hour sounds terribly slow, but is not uncommon when you include stoppages. The larger the group, the slower the ride, as the chances of stoppages increase.

Route text

The route description is written as briefly and succinctly as possible, as this helps in following the text when on the ride. The many abbreviations used are explained in the 'Route Text Abbreviations', and soon become familiar.

Maps – Ordnance Survey (OS)

If you wish to complete all the routes in this guide, you should have the latest editions of these maps: Ordnance Survey

Landranger 1:50,000 scale sheets 178, 179, 188, 189 (2cm = 1km) as they are the most up-to-date series. These can be bought from good book stores and will cost less than twenty pounds, which is less than most single components on your bike (and they should last a lot longer).

A more serious commitment, and one that I do not recommend, would be to purchase dozens of Ordnance Survey Pathfinder 1:25,000 scale sheets (4cm = 1km).

Each route lists the maps required to cover it and more map information is provided in the 'Route Index Map' and 'Route Summary Chart'. You will notice that I use kilometres for distance. This is the most appropriate measure when using these maps. Conversion to miles is achieved by multiplying by 0.6214 or multiplying by 5 and then dividing by 8.

Sketch-maps – Guidebook
These maps are of varying scales, but none smaller than 1:100,000. The emphasis is on showing clearly the route in relation to major features on the ground. They are not intended for use without the route text or an Ordnance Survey map.

Route transposition
Before setting out you should read the route description, study the route map and copy the route onto your Ordnance Survey map. This is achieved to great effect using a highlighter pen. I recommend that you take the Ordnance Survey map as well as the guide on the ride, as this enables you to deal with any perceived ambiguities in the text and also to take diversions, through curiosity or necessity. Routes can be reversed, but the text is only written for one direction.

19

ROUTE TEXT ABBREVIATIONS

L	Left	RUPP	Road Used as a Public Path
R	Right		
TL	Turn Left	RD	Road
TR	Turn Right	BRWAY	Bridleway
VL	Veer Left	BOAT	Byway Open to All Traffic
VR	Veer Right		
FL	Fork Left	XRDS	Cross Roads
FR	Fork Right	XTKS	Cross Tracks
HL	Half Left	NT	National Trust
HR	Half Right	FC	Forestry Commission
LH	Left-Hand		
RH	Right-Hand	km	Kilometres
90L	90 Degrees Turn Left	m	Metres
		N	North
90R	90 Degrees Turn Right	S	South
		E	East
SA	Straight Across/ Ahead	W	West

HOW TO COMPLETE A ROUTE

Accommodation

For accommodation, refer to tourist information offices, Youth Hostel Associations, camping guidebooks or the Ordnance Survey tourist information symbols which are found on their maps.

Getting to the start

As a certain skill has to be developed in order to navigate these routes, it is appropriate to give a six figure grid reference for the start of each route, and expect you to navigate to the start using Ordnance Survey maps or a road atlas. The starts are selected with regard to carparks but you can select an alternative start point. Park carefully, putting some money in any honesty boxes that may exist in carparks.

Network SouthEast have an extensive railway network in the county, and bicycles can be carried for free without prior booking. Off-peak tickets are available after 0930 Mondays to Fridays and any time at the weekend. Network cards are available for discounted travel, and credit card booking is available. For all enquiries and bookings, telephone 0732 770111. Train timetables can be picked up for free at the stations. The rail network and stations are clearly shown on Ordnance Survey maps.

Safety and security
Although not a mountainous county, Kent still has areas of remote, exposed and unfrequented countryside. Weather is changeable and information can be obtained from Weather-call on 0891 500402. Even in populated areas, a small problem can manifest itself into something quite serious. Make sure that you and your party are fit and well in body, bike and mind. Ride safely and do not take unnecessary risks. Always remember to inform someone of your route and estimated time of return, particularly if you are riding on your own. Take care on all roads – even the quietest lanes can attract fast drivers, so stay well into the side and do not ride two abreast. Follow the highway code and use bike lights and reflectors and reflective clothing at night. Theft often occurs in carparks, so check that your car and its contents are secure before leaving it. If you leave your bike outside a pub, for example, then lock it up.

EQUIPMENT AND SKILLS

Equipment considerations

A lot can be written about equipment, and consequently it is the subject of many specialist books. Although knowledge can be gained from these, it is best to learn through experience. I will just headline the main considerations.

Bike: Correct size frame, well-maintained, safe and fit for purpose.

Helmet: Wear the correct size and specification.

Tools: The size of tool kit should reflect your level of preparation. If your bike is well-maintained then you can carry less tools. A typical kit will include: pump, inner tube, tyre levers, puncture repair kit, small adjustable wrench, chain splitter, crank extractor, hexagonal keys, a small screwdriver and a piece of coat-hanger wire. Tools are best carried in a saddlebag.

Clothing: Appropriate for the conditions, spare clothes for wild weather.

First-aid kit: Should include field dressings, various band-ages, plasters and adhesive fabric tape.

Food and water: Take plenty for the ride. Eat and drink frequently.

Bike computer: These help greatly with estimation of time and distance.

Other items: Map, guidebook, compass, whistle, torch, rucksack or bumbag.

Personal identification: In the event of an accident, it is important to know whether a patient is: asthmatic, diabetic, allergic to penicillin or has a rare blood group. A contact address and contact telephone number could also help.

Maintenance

Another subject of many specialist books on the market. Maintenance skills come with experience, and even the best mechanics cannot anticipate some of the damage that occurs on a ride – so be prepared to improvise. Good maintenance starts with a clean bike and some knowledge of how to strip and re-assemble key parts. Ensure that all bearings have the correct amount of play, that the brakes work effectively, and that wheels and tyres are in good condition.

Map and compass work

This is an essential part of navigating these routes success-fully, and must be developed as a skill. Refer to specialist books or courses on the subject, if you feel you need more skills. Alternatively, set out on the routes at a slow attentive pace, and teach yourself. The recommended OS maps all have a comprehensive key that shows all symbols in use, and there is also a description of how to take six-figure grid references contained in the key. These references are occa-sionally used in the route descriptions to help in transposing the route onto your OS map.

Most of the legal rights of way are marked, but if in doubt, retrace your steps to your last known point and start again. As you become more familiar with the OS maps and navigation, you can explore further rights of way marked on the map, and design your own routes. Remember that the routes in this guide are not exclusively marked on the ground. This guide merely uses existing rights of way, most of which are waymarked with signposts, sign stones and arrows.

Compass work is rarely required in Kent, but is sometimes the only way to get out of a complex situation confidently, (e.g. completely disorientated in a large forest). So learn to read a compass, on its own, and with a map.

Once you are familiar with the map, you will be able to plan your ride more skilfully and make accurate estimates of time and distance.

Accidents and first aid

You should be familiar with the procedures for dealing with an accident and treating a patient, whether yourself or a partner. I do not intend to cover this subject widely here, as there are many professional sources of information readily available. In the event of an accident, the following procedure should be followed:

- Remain calm. Protect the casualty from any immediate danger. If there is a spare group member then send him/her for help.
- Check the airway is clear if the patient is unconscious.
- Stop any bleeding.
- Attend to any other injuries.
- Keep them warm and comfortable.
- Get help, when you have done everything possible.

Typical injuries after a serious crash are broken bones, cuts, concussion, shock and cramp. In nearly twenty years of cycling and ten years of mountain biking, I have never had a serious injury. Accidents result from trying to exceed your skill threshold, being reckless or just damned unlucky! More common are heat exhaustion and exposure, both of which you can experience in Kent. Learn to recognise the symptoms.

Bike handling

Only modest handling skills are required to cycle these routes. If the going gets tough you can just get off, carry and push. The main skills are those of balance, careful braking, weight distribution and gear selection, and by doing these routes you will soon have these skills sorted.

Ground conditions

Certain techniques and equipment are required to negotiate some of Kent's wonderful natural attributes.

Mud: Often clay-like and extremely sticky, and can become quite infuriating when combined with deep horse-hoof pools and autumn leaves. To prevent your bike from grinding to a halt, here are some useful tips:

- Remove mudguards.
- Keep chain well-lubricated.
- Select tyres that ensure traction but shed mud.
- Take a piece of coat-hanger wire to extract mud and leaves.
- Ensure there is no clutter around your forks, brakes and stays.
- Fit a 'Crudclaw' (cleans rear gears) and anti-chainsuck device if necessary.
- Adapt your riding style; correct gear selection, put your foot down on slippery downhill turns or cambers.

Thorns: The most common cause of punctures in Kent. Always take a spare tube, and consider some form of puncture proof material in the tyre. Remember always to inspect the tyre before re-assembling after a puncture repair, and take care not to split your finger as you do this – these thorns are big! Look out for bushes as you cycle, and beware of hedges that have recently been cut as their thorns stay hard even on the ground, into the winter.

Flints: The second most common cause of punctures in Kent, and a common cause of laceration if you crash. In the autumn, they are further disguised by the colours of the fallen leaves. A good reason for wearing a helmet and taking a field dressing in your first-aid kit.

Wet chalk and rain ruts: Although chalk absorbs water readily, it is extremely slippery when wet. Combined with the meandering rain-worn ruts that run down from the hills, you can end up spending more time on your side, than on the bike. Take care.

Sand: In many places, such as in the Weald, sand is common on path surfaces, and provides some entertaining riding when soft, and superb riding when hard. You will encounter both conditions with these routes.

Vegetation: Brambles are common in the summer, and if the path has not been cleared, they can make life rather painful. You may choose to wear long trousers, if the undergrowth is high. Also, some protection from hay fever will be necessary for sufferers.

Trees: If they are vertical, they are normally not a problem. However, since the hurricane of 1987, many areas of the south east have not been cleared, or the odd damaged tree topples – so look out for fallen trees and branches across tracks. Tree roots and rootstocks can also be exposed and rather slippery when wet.

ABOUT KENT

History
Kent, the gateway to England, has had much attention. Its quiet beauty belies the dramatic events that have shaped its history, and it has more forms of defence than any other county. The Romans first visited in 55 BC. Their attempted invasion at Deal in East Kent with over 10,000 men was repelled both by Cassilvelaunus' (the Belgic King) army and a storm that prevented the horsemen from landing. A year later they returned with a much larger force, and penetrated to Hertfordshire, where the King resigned himself to paying taxes to Rome. After 100 years of peaceful trading, the applecart was upset by the succeeding Belgic King, Cunobelinus, who raided France occasionally, so Claudius of Rome decided to occupy Kent.

The army landed at Richborough (Ritupiae): Cunobelinus' sons bravely strove to defend their land but both fell in battle, the last stand being taken by Caractacus on the banks of the River Medway. The Romans then spread throughout the rest of England.

The Romans established forts along the Saxon Shore. These were at Reculver, Richborough, Dover and Lympne, and roads ran from them to Canterbury, then along Watling

Street to Rochester and London (now the A2 road).

By the year 449 the Romans had given up on Britain, leaving Vortigern in power. He foolishly gave the Isle of Thanet to the Jutish Kings, Hengist and Horsa. Hengist slew Horsa and took Kent. Their legacy remains in much of Kent's Saxon folklore. Christianity was re-introduced to pagan Britain by Saint Augustine in 597 when he and his monks landed near Sandwich. They met King Ethelbert at Canterbury, converted him and built an abbey there.

Other invasions came to Kent, and it was occupied at some point by both the Angles and the Saxons. Eventually, the county was occupied, in the 9th century, by the Wessex King, Egbert. However, the Danes started to take their winter holidays on the islands of Thanet and Sheppey. In 851 they stayed and occupied Kent. The next invasion started in Sussex, not Kent, for a change. This was the Norman Conquest.

After some settling, Kent entered a prosperous era. The location of Canterbury Cathedral attracted many visitors from around the world, especially to the tomb of Thomas A'Becket. Their gifts added to the prosperity. In the 11th and 12th centuries, both the abbey and the cathedral were burnt down. The abbey was never rebuilt, but the cathedral was, in stone imported from Caen in France.

Kent has not been invaded since these times, although there have been many threats of invasion. Henry II inaugurated the Cinque Ports (pronounced 'sank' – French for five), and granted charters if the townspeople manned boats in case of attack. These ports are Sandwich (the oldest), Dover, Hythe, Romney and Hastings. Old Romney was landlocked when a great storm in 1287 diverted the River Rother. Subsidiary to the Cinque Ports were Deal, Folkestone,

Rye, Winchelsea (then an island) and Tenterden (now 17 kilometres inland! Its harbour was at Small Hythe).

Henry VIII installed the first co-ordinated line of defence since the Romans, in the form of Tudor castles and block-houses between Kent and Cornwall. These are to be found at Deal, Walmer, Sandown and Sandgate. Walmer is now the official residence of the Lord Warden of the Cinque Ports – The Queen Mother. In Napoleonic times, Martello towers and incredible fortresses were built, virtually all of which survive today. Those in Chatham represent the greatest examples in Europe.

The two world wars have left their mark on the county. The landscape and buildings were ravaged, not only by direct bombing from aircraft, V bombs and shore batteries; but also, as bombers were chased by fighters they would jettison their loads on Kent, peppering the land with bombholes.

The Battle of Britain took place over Kent, and many landmarks are evidence of this event. Also to be found are pill boxes, gun emplacements, bomb shelters, aerodromes, and other more covert constructions, supposedly including a nuclear defence operations centre under Dover Castle.

Geology and geography

South-east England was once at the bottom of the sea in the Cretacious period. The predominant chalk has been formed by minute sea creatures. The sea surface was forced up as an anticline or dome. This chalk dome was eroded in its centre by rain and rivers until the weaker sands inside were exposed, thus creating the wealden clay vale, until reaching the harder rocks of the Greensand Ridge and Forest Ridge. The rivers that had run off the dome remained, and cut their path through the steep chalk scarp downs that typify the northern and southern areas.

Kent is bisected by the North Downs. These hills rise to 800 feet in places. Many sunken paths exist on the Downs where iron shod hooves and wheels have broken down the surface, allowing it to be washed away over the years. Much of Kent is an area of natural beauty (AONB) with much of the Downs, Weald and cliffs included. The Downs have very few streams, even in the steepest valleys, due to the absorbent nature of the chalk surface, and Kent relies on much of its water supply from the underlying water-table.

North Kent has extensive marshes that bound the Thames Estuary, and contain numerous valleys running off the dip slope of the North Downs. Much of the coastline of Kent has changed considerably, even in recent years, due to the erosive effects of the sea, and the continuing oscillations of land and sea height.

East Kent is a land of sheer cliffs, and was once connected to France before sea action broke through.

Central Kent, south of Maidstone, is very low lying with good drainage.

South Kent contains Romney Marsh, an area over 500km^2, often known as 'The eighth continent', as it is so different from anywhere else in the country. The landscape was created by the changing heights of land and sea and the subsequent reclamation of the marshland, which started as soon as long shore drift caused the great shingle banks at Dungeness.

Human geography
With over 70% of its boundary exposed to the sea, Kent has many of its largest communities on the coast. Early settlers

ventured inland up the river systems to establish Canterbury and Maidstone. Much less progress was made into the Weald, as it was regarded as a dark and forbidding place due to the amount of forest. Only the River Medway provided easy navigation. A classification still in use today came from this period – Kentish men, west of the river and men of Kent, east of the river.

The forests were depleted to aid the massive Victorian shipbuilding industry. Some of the forest remnants still contain evidence of the former industries that they supported. Furnace or hammer ponds used to provide a head of water for the waterwheel-driven forging hammers of the steel workers – cannons and the railings for St Paul's Cathedral were made here. The charcoal burners provided the fuel from their coppiced woods to fire the forges.

Rudyard Kipling lived in the Weald from 1902 to 1936 at Batemans, Burwash in East Sussex, and he wrote:

(Out of the Weald, the secret Weald,
Men sent in ancient years,
The horse-shoes red at Flodden Field,
The arrows at Poitiers!)

Kent had a great history in shipbuilding both in wood and steel at Chatham dockyard until it closed in 1982. Also, with cement production, Kent had the biggest chalk quarrying operations in the world at the turn of the century.

The earliest of the chalk workings were called 'dene-holes'. These were shafts sunk through the soil layer on top of the Downs in order to reach quality chalk beneath, whereby a three-lobed excavation would take place. Sometimes, the

31

shafts can still be found uncovered, about 2m in diameter and seemingly bottomless, as some reached 100 feet deep. Some farmers use them to tip rubbish into, and it appears that they will not manage to fill them up in their lifetime! Dene-holes are virtually exclusive to the North Downs in Kent and are over 200 years old.

East Kent even had a coal industry. Tapping very deep seams, when operating, it supplied 1% of the UK's coal. The mines have long since closed down, and little evidence of their workings remains. The industries with most impact are those of cement and papermaking, with their associated chimneys and wharves.

Today the leading industries are agriculture, manufacturing and tourism. These are aided by the ferry terminals at Dover, Sheerness, Margate and Folkestone.

The county's comprehensive rail and road network connects the major towns to London, the M2 and M20 motorways being the main arteries. This greatly enhances swift travel through the county in east-west, west-east directions. North-south, south-north is considerably slower. The latest transport addition is the Channel Tunnel, with its associated high speed rail link, which is to run beside the North Downs. This railway will provide fast commuter and business links with France and London, and is intended to reduce truck traffic.

Agriculture
A variety of farming exists in Kent, as the parcels and type of land vary considerably. Arable farming of cereal is common in the more fertile central and dip slope areas. Much of the woodland on the Downs and Forest Ridge is coppiced. Coppicing is a process whereby broadleaved trees such as

oak, ash, birch and hazel are felled, allowing them to sprout shoots again from the dormant buds in the stump. These grow into poles and are used by coopers, tanners, wheelwrights and charcoal burners.

Pastoral farming is most common on the less fertile areas of the North Downs and Romney Marsh. Dairy farming is adjacent to this industry.

Market gardening and fruit farming is to be found on the lower areas adjacent to the River Thames and the River Medway, and it is this industry that gave the county its title of the 'garden of England'. Hops (Humulus Lupulus) are commonplace for the real ale market, and vineyards are becoming more successful with some Kentish wines now winning European applause and prizes.

Weather and climate
Kent is virtually the sunniest, but not quite the driest county in England. Annual rainfall is about 30 inches. Droughts in the summer are often succeeded by heavy rainfall in autumn. The most exposed areas to wind tend to be on the coast, especially on the cliff tops and marshes. Prevailing wind is generally south-westerly. On lower ground, mists are common with heavy frosts in the winter.

Flora and fauna
Surprisingly, there are more indigenous trees in south-east England than in Scotland, even with the loss of 10 million trees in the 1987 hurricane. The countryside really comes alive in the spring with the emergence of daffodils, bluebells and apple blossom. The patchwork extends in the summer with oilseed rape, lavender and poppy fields to complement the cocktail of colours and smells from the fruit fields. On

33

rough pastures, such as the south-facing North Downs, rabbits, pheasants, butterflies and wild flowers become commonplace.

Architecture

Most buildings are of brick, even some of the oldest, as brick clay has been available for centuries from the Thames Estuary marshes. Other buildings are typically timber-framed houses or weather boarded, sometimes with cat-slide roofs (roofs that nearly reach the ground). Older roofs often use peg tiles, held in place by two wooden pegs each. Quaint pubs tucked down quiet lanes are often some of the oldest buildings.

The most noticeable building format is that of the oast-house. These are designed for kiln drying or roasting the hops used to make real ale. The buildings are characterised by their spires topped with a wooden cowling that rotates to face the wind, in order to ventilate the roasting process. Oast-houses may be of a single spire, single building format, or multi-spired rows of buildings. The Whitbread hop farm near Maidstone is the biggest in the country, with dozens of oast-houses.

ROUTE MAP SYMBOLS

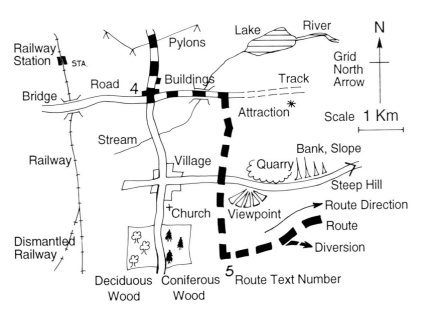

ROUTE 1 - PENSHURST

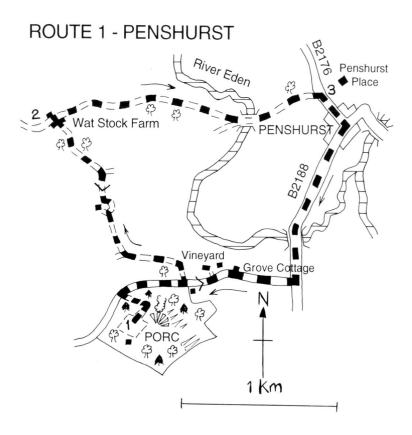

ROUTE 1 – PENSHURST

Introduction

A very special, short route is provided here because the facilities at Penshurst are a fine distraction from a longer ride on local roads and bridleways. The Penshurst Off Road Club (PORC) operates from a 40 acre wood overlooking the village of Penshurst in the upper Medway valley. Mike Westphal owns the wood, and over the last few years he has developed a mountain biking paradise. There are downhill courses on the steep, wooded hills with ramps, jumps and berms, a trials playground in a quarry and a flatter plateau for easy riding along rhododendron lined trails.

The area is particularly suitable for parents to take their children to learn to cycle off road. The centre even arranges for group tuition. Riders should first check in at Grove Cottage at 519429 then proceed to the carpark at 513427. A discount is offered to all holders of this book. The entry fee is very reasonable. For more information ring Mike on 0892 870136.

Sustrans would like to create a route connecting PORC to Tonbridge via Penshurst Place and the Eden Valley Park. This would be part of a wider network to Maidstone and the Medway Towns. This would also link with the nearby Forest Way and Worth Way railway paths, and thus to Gatwick Airport.

Grade: Easy
Duration: 1hr
Distance: 7km
Ascent: 130m
Maps: 188
Links: None
Start: PORC carpark in the woods of South Park at 513427.

Alternative starts: None
Refreshments: Several pubs in the lanes just off route, or in Penshurst. Many tearooms in Penshurst. Wine tasting and other refreshments at the vineyard.
Care: It is easy to go completely bananas in the PORC grounds. Serious racers have done serious damage to themselves and their bikes here.

Attractions on route
Penshurst Place: Home of Viscount De L'Isle, built in 1341 with extensive gardens.
Vineyard: Wine tasting for the grown-ups and an adjacent rare breeds farm for the kids. What more could you want?

Attractions off route
Hever Castle: A romantic 13th century moated castle, once the home of Anne Boleyn, with a 35 acre lake, maze, gardens and hamlet.
Chiddingstone Village: A quaint main street, church and castle. The Chiding Stone is a large sandstone rock behind the main street and nagging wives were once brought here to be chided by the villagers.
Tonbridge: A busy town with the River Medway and a castle.

Above Tonbridge is the Bidborough Ridge, a superb place to view the Greensand Ridge and the Medway valley.
Royal Tunbridge Wells: Known for The Pantiles and Spa.
Rock climbing: Popular area for this pursuit, with some sandstone outcrops up to 15m high. Most popular are High Rocks at 558382, Harrison's Rocks at 533365 and Bowles at 542330.
Ashdown Forest: With few bridleways and strictly no cycling, the Ashdown Forest in East Sussex is an incredibly frustrating place to visit with a mountain bike. However, there are numerous carparks, and a good, hard road ride. The forest is mainly open moor and is over 200m high in places. The real Pooh Bridge is in the Ashdown Forest, as A. A. Milne lived here.

Route Description
1. From the PORC carpark return to the RD. TR and travel downhill for 200m to BRWAY on L. TL down tarmac and FR to the entrance of a house. TR before the gate (lions) to follow a fenced path around a house to a tarmac road. Follow uphill to FL at top. At Wat Stock Farm TR on Eden Valley Walk. BRWAY.

2. Go downhill on a good double track through a gate and down to a tarmac RD. TL (SA) to reach B2176. (Opposite is Penshurst Place).

3. TR, and ride into Penshurst. TR at T-junction out of village and over bridge. TR at vineyard sign uphill past Grove Cottage back to PORC.

Extensions and Diversions
The centre of the Ashdown Forest is less than 20km away by road. A 12km road ride will link you with Route 2 – Ide Hill.

39

ROUTE 2 - IDE HILL

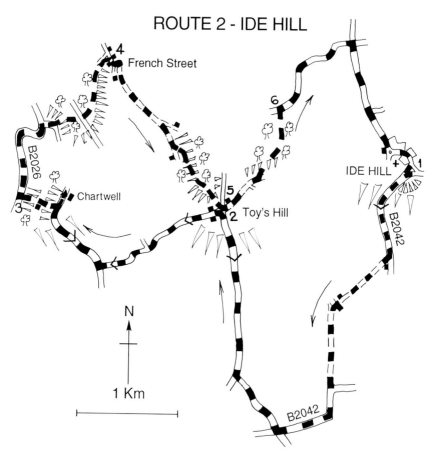

French Street

B2026

Chartwell

3

Toy's Hill

5

2

6

IDE HILL

B2042

B2042

N

1 Km

ROUTE 2 – IDE HILL

Introduction
An area with many of the characteristics of the very popular Surrey Hills, but much quieter. The wooded, sandy hills provide some technical riding with both steep ascents and descents. A short and hard route, in an area that has much potential for further exploration.

Grade: Difficult
Duration: 3hrs
Distance: 17km
Ascent: 530m
Maps: 188
Links: None
Start: Ide Hill carpark at 488517.

Alternative starts: Toy's Hill NT carpark at 469516.
Refreshments: Shops, pubs and garage at Ide Hill.
Care: Do not be tempted to go fast down the steep and narrow single tracks – you may meet other users.

Attractions on route
Ide Hill Village: An idyllic green with church, pubs, garage and shop.
Views: From the start point great views of the Medway valley, Bough Beech Reservoir, and Ashdown Forest on the horizon.

43

Page 41: Approaching French Street

Chartwell: Sir Winston Churchill's home from 1924. The house has unusual crows foot gable-ends and a gridded façade.

French Street: Delightful hamlet at end of road, in quiet valley.

Attractions off route

Hanging Bank and Brockhoult Mount: A 97 acre wood with carpark and views at 497518.

Dryhill: A carpark in a ragstone quarry with a shelter, picnic area and toilet at 498552.

Emmetts Garden: Landscaped gardens with extensive views at 476525.

Toy's Hill: NT carpark in 320 acre wood at 469516.

Route Description

1. Travel S downhill on B2042 for 1km then TR on BRWAY through gate at side of house. Go downhill on remote tarmac past cottage and then through farms. Eventually VL to B2042 at 481495. TR (SA), TR, and TR again soon steeply uphill to Toy's Hill.

2. TL at XRDS in Toy's Hill. This road soon takes you steeply downhill to reach T-junction at 457508. TR steeply uphill to BRWAY on L after 800m. (Chartwell is just ahead). TL up good double track to single track across driveway. Follow LH edge to descend steep, rocky track to B2026 at 448515. (The route goes off the map here for a few minutes).

3. TR and follow RD downhill around bends to take next R at T-junction. Where this RD bends sharp R after 100m, take steep BRWAY single track uphill to RD at 456522. Cross over RD through gate on BRWAY, double to single track. VL down to lane. Stop. Turn sharp R back away from lane on BRWAY, soon between two large hedges to RD and hamlet of French Street.

4. TR and FL steeply down to French Street Farm on BRWAY. Then travel uphill out of valley on RD to FL by gate. Go uphill on single track, (Greensand Way). VL up very steep hill, then another hill, following waymark posts to flat summit. Follow more posts downhill. VR (CARE) through gorse. Eventually VL steeply down (CARE) to RD and the XRDS you came to earlier.

5. TL (cross) and SA on a RD marked dead-end. Follow tarmac down and up to FL and L again before gate. Continue on BRWAY single track soon to double, stony track up steep hill. Follow this up and down then TR out of valley eventually to RD at 475526.

6. TR, and follow RD to XRDS. TR, and follow RD into Ide Hill village. Through village, downhill then FR back to carpark.

Extensions and Diversions
A 5km road ride will link you with Route 3 – Plaxtol 1. A 12km road ride will link you with Route 1 – Penshurst and PORC.

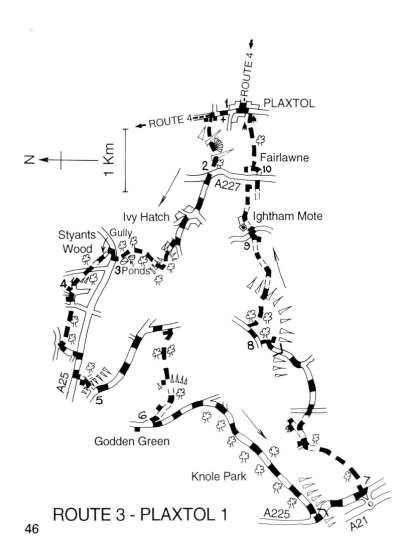

ROUTE 4

1 PLAXTOL

← ROUTE 4

Fairlawne

2

A227

10

Ivy Hatch

Ightham Mote

9

Styants Wood

Gully

3 Ponds

4

8

A25

5

6

Godden Green

7

Knole Park

A225

A21

N ← 1 Km

ROUTE 3 - PLAXTOL 1

ROUTE 3 – PLAXTOL 1

Introduction
An intricate and hard route on the Greensand Ridge that runs
alongside the massive Knole Park. There are a few technical
sections that provide just reward if you can clear them all in
the one ride. This route can be linked with Route 4 – Plaxtol 2
– to create a very demanding figure-of-eight route.

Grade: Difficult
Duration: 3.5hrs
Distance: 27km
Ascent: 640m
Maps: 188
Links: Route 4 – Plaxtol 2
Start: Plaxtol. Plenty of parking in the village main street
at 605535.

Alternative starts: Godden Green or carpark at Styants
Wood, 578558.
Refreshments: Several pubs on route, with the Bucks Head at
Godden Green and a garage at Plaxtol.
Care: Horse-riders are common in this area. Rocky and sandy
sections also common, so dismount if unsure of your ability.

Attractions on route
Oldbury Hill and Styants Wood: 150 acres of wood at over
200m, forming the southern half of a massive Iron Age hill

fort, built about 100 BC, and fortified by the Belgae.

Knole Park: A 1,000 acre deer park owned by the Sackville family open to pedestrians only. In the centre of the park is the largest private house in England, which appears to be more like a whole village with the many tiled roofs hidden behind the main façade and walled gardens. It has 365 rooms, 52 staircases and a renowned collection of 14th century furniture. The park has extensive woodland, and the devastation after the 1987 hurricane was much publicised. Jack Cade defeated the King's army here in the 1450 rebellion. It is sad that bikes are not allowed in this beautiful park.

Ightham Mote: An impressive 14th century moated manor house with great hall, chapel and crypt. The route passes right past the moated side of the house.

Fairlawne: A delightful house with landscaped gardens. The route passes through these on a bridleway.

Attractions off route

Dene Park, Shipbourne: A 220 acre wood of mixed hardwood and conifer.

One Tree Hill: 34 acres of NT wood with extensive views over the Medway valley.

Sevenoaks: A busy town, named after the magnificent seven oaks on the green. All but one were lost in the hurricane, so rather than change the town's name to Anoak, six new young oaks were planted in their place.

Route Description

1. From village main street, go W and uphill to top. TR and FR past church on L. SA past T-junction on R then TL between houses on a BRWAY uphill. Cycle through orchard and alongside the hedge, then across field past copse on R to another hedge. TR to follow LH edge of field. At the L corner join track through woods to a gate and the A227.

2. Take great care crossing this busy road. Continue SA on RD through Ivy Hatch with pub on R and TL at fork. TR at next R then immediately TL up BRWAY. This is a sandy, technical ascent to the top and a clearing. After a few metres TR down steep BRWAY winding on a single track in sand. Pass ponds on L to arrive at A25.

3. Cross and TR then TL into layby with wooden posts. TL sharply on BRWAY up bank then down gully to RD at 578559. Cross RD and follow BRWAY single track over XTKS through wood. Soon climb steeply up technical gully to tarmac and cottage. Up and over then down to RD.

4. TR, and at T-junction head SA on BRWAY, in woods, with fence on R to RD. TL to A25. TR, and after 400m, TL at entrance to Coldhanger on tarmac BRWAY. Soon FR down through rhododendron bushes, steeply down BRWAY to drive and RD.

5. TL and follow RD uphill for over 1km, to TR on RD before pub. Soon TR on BRWAY at 569545 on a stony track. Descend technical rocky gutter and continue across fields to R of gate in hedge. Go steeply up past cottage onto double track past White House and down to RD at Godden Green.

6. TL at RD before Bucks Head pub. After 1km FR on RD then VR and SA to A225 (Knole Park on the R). TL down steep hill to FL at bottom.

7. TL sharp, around cottage to follow a RUPP on undulating double track. After over 1km just before gate and oast-houses, TR, now on BRWAY. Continue on downhill single track to double track past big 'triffid' plant to RD. SA at this T-junction and continue on RD. At 90R TL uphill (dead-end RD). Continue on tarmac steeply to gate, then up BRWAY. Climb rocky hill to Rooks Hill House and gate on L at 566532.

8. TR on tarmac for 300m, then TR on BRWAY. After 200m FL down and up then down long descent past gates on R. Travel down again to eventually VL through farm to gates and RD.

9. TR, then after 50m, TL through gates on BRWAY and pass to the R of Ightham Mote. Climb up past carpark, across fields on double track to single track past BRWAY on L to gate. Cycle into grazing field, and TR down to gates at lane. TL to gate and A227.

10. Cross over A227 and go SA into Fairlawne. Go through gate, on BRWAY down drive through gardens. Then VR before buildings to gate and grazing fields. Into fields and cross, following yellow posts, on a sheep trod path through gates, with woods on R and fir trees on L. Then travel down avenue of trees to gates at RD. TL back to Plaxtol.

Extensions and Diversions

A 5km road ride will link you with Route 2 – Ide Hill. A 12km road ride will link you with Route 1 – Penshurst and PORC.

Climbing away from Plaxtol

Orchard beneath Mereworth Woods (Plaxtol 2)

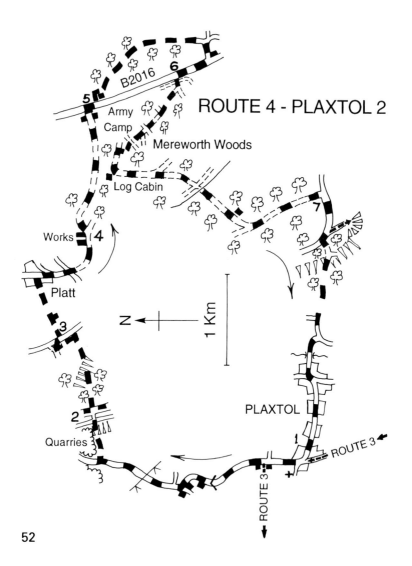

ROUTE 4 - PLAXTOL 2

B2016

Army Camp

Mereworth Woods

Log Cabin

Works

Platt

N ← 1 Km

Quarries

PLAXTOL

ROUTE 3

ROUTE 3

ROUTE 3

5

6

7

4

3

2

1

ROUTE 4 – PLAXTOL 2

Introduction

Near the very end of the Greensand Ridge rises a plateau with a massive area of woodland, and an international size air station, now decommissioned. The Greensand Way passes nearby on its way to Yalding. This route rises and falls through orchards out of Plaxtol and takes a course through the deep woodland of Mereworth, some of which is a military training area. It can be linked with Route 3 – Plaxtol 1, to create a very demanding figure-of-eight route.

Grade: Moderate
Duration: 2.5hrs
Distance: 18km
Ascent: 300m
Maps: 188
Links: Route 3 – Plaxtol 1
Start: Plaxtol. Plenty of parking in the village main street at 605535.

Alternative starts: Platt village.
Refreshments: Pubs on route, shops and garage at Plaxtol. Just off route is the excellent Artichoke pub at Hamptons, 625523.
Care: In the military area, do not stray from the bridleways as you may encounter the enemy! There is a very active

presence here, and they will see and hear you before you see them. Tripwires and night activities are common.

Attractions on route
Mereworth Woods: A vast wood, actively coppiced. The central part is an army training area. I spent much of my youth here.

Attractions off route
Old Soar Manor: A 13th century house with solar block. Free admission.
West Malling Air Station: This was the venue for an annual air show until recently.

Route Description
1. From the main street of Plaxtol go W uphill to TR at the top and FR past church on L. SA on undulating RD, ignoring turns to T-junction at 599548. TR and follow RD SA under pylons to quarries. TR on BRWAY. Descend to the RD.

2. Cross grass and another RD and a carpark before entering the woods. Follow the valley floor past sewage works to VL up through wood to RH field edge. Follow this fenced path along field edge, then TL and continue parallel to RD uphill to track by gate. TR and FR to RD at 615564.

3. TR here, then take BRWAY on L, on track to left of building through orchards to RD at Platt. TR and SA to reach staggered junction and continue SA towards Invicta Site. VL past field on R. Then go SA past works on L now on BRWAY and into wood on track to gate at 628559.

4. Through gate, TL and follow good track. VR uphill then undulating past scout camp and kennels to B2016.

5. TR and soon TL on BRWAY past Longwall House to grass area. TR back on yourself behind gardens along undulating section in wood, ignoring all turns to RD. TR back to B2016. TR for 300m.

6. TL, through gate on BRWAY into training area. SA track on track to FR following waymarks across forest. Continue on tracks and roads for 1.5km to a log cabin at 634557. VL on RD uphill away from cabin for 300m. Then FR at waymark to follow dirt track soon to reach main track. VL then sharp R through hedge and out of training area. Follow track for 1km to gate then past house on L to reach main track. TL here and follow the BRWAY to the road at 633533.

7. TR for a short distance to T-junction. TR and after 200m TL on BOAT down stony double track to FR and then down stony single track to RD. TL here (SA) and take second R down over stream to T-junction. TL and SA uphill back into Plaxtol.

Extensions and Diversions
A 5km road ride will link you with Route 5 – Trosley.

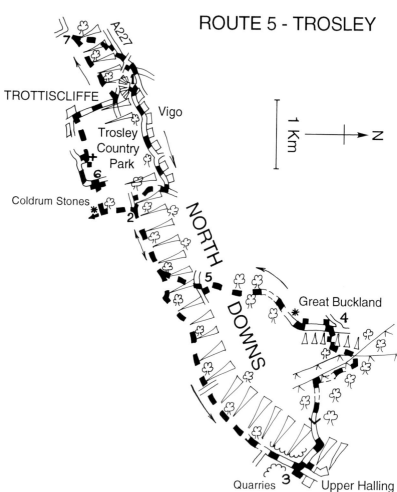

ROUTE 5 - TROSLEY

A227

7

TROTTISCLIFFE

Vigo

Trosley
Country
Park

1 Km

N

6

Coldrum Stones

2

NORTH

DOWNS

5

Great Buckland

4

3

Quarries

Upper Halling

ROUTE 5 – TROSLEY

Introduction

A fairly hard route that captures the true character of the North Downs, with beech and oak trees covering both the steep scarp slope and intricate deep valleys of the dip slope. There are many views of the Medway valley, and some technical sections in mud and on ancient flint cart tracks. Trosley is the correct pronunciation of Trottiscliffe!

Grade: Moderate
Duration: 3hrs
Distance: 21km
Ascent: 500m
Maps: 178 or 188
Links: None
Start: Trosley Country Park carpark at 633611.

Alternative starts: Trottiscliffe or Upper Halling villages. Holly Hill carpark at 670630.

Refreshments: There are two pubs in Upper Halling – the Black Boy and the Pilgrims Rest. The Vigo on the A227 with a fruit shop opposite, and shops in both villages above.

Care: Horse-riders are active in this area.

Attractions on route

Trosley Country Park: A 160 acre area of downland kept pruned by sheep and rabbits. There is an information centre, toilet, and carpark with small fee. No cycling is allowed in the park.

Whitehorse Wood: Large woods once occupied by a US army camp in WWII. Remnants still remain – a water tower and some concrete foundations, that you cross on route.

Halling: Massive quarries still actively mined. The chalk is used for the production of cement at Snodland, hence the tall chimney. Across the river can be seen numerous old quarries, (over 100 years old) many of which are still owned by Blue Circle PLC.

Dode: Nothing remains of the village except the church at 668637, a grim reminder of the devastating effects of the plague. The church may unfortunately become a private house.

Coldrum Long Barrow: A neolithic tomb similar and symmetrically opposite to Kit's Coty House across the river at Blue Bell Hill. Dated at 2500 BC, the barrow was excavated in 1910 and the remains of 22 bodies were found.

Attractions off route

Luddesdown Village: A delightful valley called the bowling alley leads to the ancient village of Luddesdown – the Celtic name gives it away. The MOD failed a few years ago to capture 600 acres for mine-laying training. Military activity passed by in 1648 when Fairfax's men marched through this valley to outflank the Royalists at Aylesford.

Holly Hill: One of Kent's highest points, a 32 acre wood with views across the Medway valley.

Paddlesworth Church: You may not mind a diversion down

the hill to visit this unusual church at 685621.

Brands Hatch: You can often hear the sound of racing from this international circuit at 575645.

Route Description

1. From Trosley Country Park entrance TR to follow Waterlow Road and then TR at Erskine Road to T-junction at 649617. TR on BOAT, flat then steep down (CARE) to base of Downs.

2. TL at RD at bottom to follow BRWAY along base of Downs. Cycle past brick building eventually down to a track junction at 666617. TL still on North Downs Way, now a RUPP on undulating path for 1.5km to RD. SA RD and then on RUPP to RD. SA between quarries towards Upper Halling.

3. At Black Boy pub TL up Chapel Lane on steep RD soon in woods deteriorating to track. TR at top through gate on flat. SA ignoring two R turns, with pylons on L. Track bottoms out then continues on BOAT. Follow field on L and at T-junction TL to follow field edge on L. Soon FL under pylons along track in wood. Leave field on L at ash track and TR down steep BRWAY (CARE) to RD at 670643.

4. TL up valley and through Great Buckland, Dode Church on R. RD turns into BOAT. SA up valley then into woods uphill to RD.

5. Cross RD and into woods on RUPP. Flat then steep flint downhill (CARE) to bottom. TR on BRWAY and follow base of Downs to RD. (This is the reverse of the outward route). TL immediately down on BRWAY to Coldrum Long Barrow on R. Retrace route 100m and TL on BRWAY eventually through gate to RD and T-junction at 649607.

Dode Church at Great Buckland

6. TL, soon 90R then TR to church. VL past church and through farm courtyard on BRWAY to RD in Trottiscliffe and T-junction. TR uphill, VL and TL on BOAT (Pilgrims Way) to nearly reach RD after 1km.

7. TR up BOAT to top of Downs past house to A227. TR, SA at XRDS past pub and take next R. Then TR into Waterlow Road and back into Trosley Country Park.

Extensions and Diversions
A 7km road ride across the motorway bridge will link you with Route 6 – Blue Bell Hill 1. A 5km road ride south will link you with Route 4 – Plaxtol 2 at Mereworth Wood. An 8km road ride will get you to Brands Hatch.

GREAT BUCKLAND

GMT

ROUTE 6 - BLUE BELL HILL 1

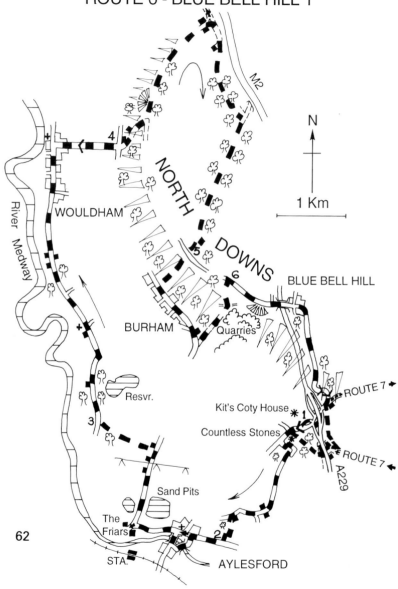

ROUTE 6 – BLUE BELL HILL 1

Introduction
This route is the harder and longer partner to Route 7 – Blue
Bell Hill 2, with which it makes a figure-of-eight for the more
ambitious rider. It covers ground that is representative of
much of the history of Kent, with chalk quarries and neolithic
stones commonplace. The Downs are climbed several times,
and the River Medway is frequent company – following this
river lends itself to more gentle cycling. Sustrans have
identified a route along the river from Maidstone to
Rochester.

Grade: Moderate
Duration: 3hrs
Distance: 25km
Ascent: 450m
Maps: 178
Links: Route 7 – Blue Bell Hill 2

Start: To reach the start: Northbound on the A229 turn off
signed Aylesford. TL at STOP sign, and cross to park in layby
opposite. Southbound on the A229 turn off signed Aylesford.
Go under A229 past Lower Bell pub to park in layby on right.
The layby is at 747606.
Alternative starts: The villages of Wouldham, Eccles, Aylesford and Blue Bell Hill all provide parking. Blue Bell Hill

picnic site provides viewpoint parking for a small fee.

Refreshments: These can be found in the villages mentioned above, at their numerous pubs and shops. Other refreshments can be found at tea vans at the start, and shops in the villages on route. Two fuel stations near the start are open 24hrs. Toilets are available at the pubs, fuel stations and at Blue Bell Hill Picnic Site. A notable pub is the Robin Hood at 734628 which has a special walkers' bar.

Care: The paths here are popular with all users, and as some are byways, other vehicles do appear, sometimes at speed.

Attractions on route

Little Kit's Coty House (or The Countless Stones): at 745603 is a collection of once standing stones, a short walk from the road, that a local baker set out to count, by putting a loaf on each as he went round. When he reached the last stone the Devil was sitting on it, and that was it, the baker was never seen again.

Aylesford Village: This appears on many postcards and is best viewed at high tide from the Bailey bridge at 731588. The Little Gem in the village is the smallest pub in Kent, and has a ridiculously low front door. Inside is an unusual balcony seating area.

The Friars: Just out of Aylesford at 724589 is an important religious centre with superb architecture and resident monks.

Wouldham/Burham/Eccles: The network of chalkpits and old industrial remains between Eccles and Wouldham once formed the largest Cement Workings in the world, with 1000 men and 80 barges. Their demise at the beginning of this century caused severe local poverty. Wouldham church contains the grave of Sir Walter Burke who was born here, and in his arms Lord Nelson died.

High Speed Rail Link: The Nashenden Valley will soon be the site of much activity, as the Channel Tunnel Rail Link will pass by here parallel to the M2, before disappearing into a tunnel above Upper Nashenden Farm. The railway re-emerges beneath the White Horse Stone, Route 7 – Blue Bell Hill 2.

Blue Bell Hill: The popular viewpoint at 743622 is a must, as it offers an unchallenged view of the Medway valley. The Upper and Lower Bell pubs are so named because, back a century, the narrow cart track that joined them on the scarp of the Downs could only accommodate one cart, so a bell was rung when one was ascending or descending thus avoiding head-on collisions or traffic jams.

Attractions off route

The Medway Towns: These towns consist of the adjacent towns of Gillingham and Chatham and the City of Rochester. They are surrounded by an impressive network of Napoleonic defences, with Amherst Redoubt the finest example of Georgian defence in the country with its gatehouse, tunnels, ditches, barracks, magazines and park. Chatham also has the most complete Georgian dockyard in the world (there is a ropery here with buildings over 1km long); and the Royal Engineers' Museum, with Medway the home of both the Sappers and the Ghurkhas. Historic Rochester has a famous cathedral and Norman castle. The keep is the tallest in the country. Rochester is well known for its Dickensian connections, and a walk along the High Street will soon bring his books to life. Rochester hosts many festivals, concerts and events throughout the year.

Kit's Coty House: at 745608 is a perfectly balanced example of a Stone Age burial chamber entrance, and is worth a walk up to, on the footpath after your ride. It is also an excellent viewpoint from which to study most of this route and the Medway valley. These stones, and The Countless Stones, are in symmetry with similar stones across the valley at Trottiscliffe visited by Route 5 – Trosley.

Museum of Kent Life at Sandling: This centre has huge renovated barns, hop fields and agricultural equipment. Nearby is Tyland barn, Sandling, a conservation centre.

M2/Medway Motorway Bridge: Until recently, this bridge had the longest pre-stressed concrete single span in Europe and at over 35m high is an impressive structure to cross. It is worth a diversion to cross it and return on its other side on the special foot/cycle paths giving views of the Medway valley to the south and Rochester with its castle and cathedral to the north. The M2 is to be widened here in a few years' time.

Route Description

1. Head W and downhill from layby towards Aylesford. Go L around adverse camber bend, past entrance to Little Kit's Coty House on the L. Take the first RD on the L. Follow this round and down for 1.5km, just past Safeway depot on L. TL on BRWAY between fences to reach RD.

2. TR and follow towards Aylesford. TL between carparks before village and over Bailey bridge. TR over old stone bridge to traffic lights. TL and up short hill then flat to go 90R opposite entrance to The Friars. Follow RD for just over 1km under pylons, then after 100m take RUPP on L past gate across fields to meet concrete road after 800m. (Beware of big trucks).

3. Continue on RD past Southern Water Works and Burham Court Church to rough track.

Magnificent barn at the Friars near Aylesford

Cycle through industrial estate to RD and then to Wouldham. SA through village, past pubs and shop. Just before church at end of village TR up School Lane to foot of Downs.

4. SA and up BOAT steeply to top of Downs. TL here on BRWAY (North Downs Way) downhill with hedge on R. Then across field (in future to cross the High Speed Rail Link) and descend down through farm. VR up to RD. (Here you can divert L to ride down to the Medway Motorway Bridge). TR to follow RD parallel to M2 up past Southern Water Works on BRWAY. Follow LH field edge then into woods to a farm, with a barking dog at 739643. TR after farm and go uphill on BRWAY, (in the future over the High Speed Rail Link) and into woods for 2km to The Robin Hood pub and RD.

5. Cross straight over the RD and down a steep rutted BOAT (CARE) to the RD at Burham. TL and pass 1km through village. Just past bus stop on L before RD turns R downhill, take BOAT on L. Pass between hedges and quarries on very wide track up into woods going SA at XTKS. Climb uphill very steeply to RD on top of Downs at 736625.

6. TR and follow RD past viewpoint on R over A229 to XRDS. SA past The Upper Bell pub. Soon 90R to follow RD flat for 1.5km then steeply downhill (CARE) to T-junction. (TL here to join Route 7 – Blue Bell Hill 2). Cross road HR and down BOAT in ditch crossing fields to fuel station. TR in front of station to go under A229 subway. TL for 50m then TR on BOAT in woods to RD junction. TR up steep hill back to layby and finish.

Extensions and Diversions
A 7km road ride over the motorway bridge will link you with Route 5 – Trosley.

ROUTE 7 - BLUE BELL HILL 2

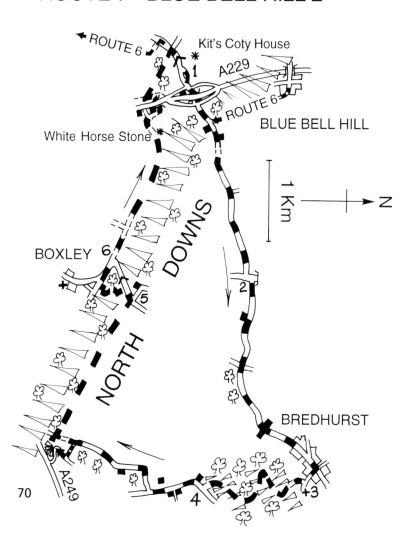

ROUTE 6

Kit's Coty House

A229

1

ROUTE 6

BLUE BELL HILL

White Horse Stone

1 Km

N

DOWNS

BOXLEY 6

5

2

NORTH

BREDHURST

70

A249

4

+3

ROUTE 7 – BLUE BELL HILL 2

Introduction

High on the North Downs, this route travels through ancient woodland on old cart tracks and follows part of the North Downs Way. Technical sections exist with mud, rocks and chalk on this route for the more advanced rider. It can be linked with Route 6 – Blue Bell Hill 1, to provide a demanding figure-of-eight ride.

Grade: Moderate
Duration: 2.5hrs
Distance: 18km
Ascent: 360m
Maps: 178 or 188
Links: Route 6 – Blue Bell Hill 1
Start: To reach the start: Northbound on the A229, turn off signed Aylesford. TL at STOP sign and cross to park in layby opposite. Southbound on the A229, turn off signed Aylesford. Go under A229 past Lower Bell pub to park in layby on right. The layby is at 747606.
Alternative starts: The villages listed below all provide parking.
Refreshments: Villages of Bredhurst, Boxley, Detling and Blue Bell Hill. Tea van in layby at start. Fuel stations on A229.
Care: A popular area with families, walkers and horse-riders.

71

Pg. 69: Steep descent in Boxley Woods

Attractions on route

White Horse Stone: Resembles a horse? Derived from Horsa, the ancient King? The White Horse of Kent? Well, it's a big sarsen stone in the wood at 753603.

High Speed Rail Link: This is due to emerge from its tunnel in the Downs just above the White Horse Stone.

Attractions off route

The Larches: An area of woodland typical of the south facing Downs. Good for a family picnic, beneath Detling Hill at 789587.

Boxley Village: A small, picturesque village with a nice pub, church, abbey and a stream claimed to be Tennyson's 'Babbling Brook'.

Maidstone: The county town has a museum, the River Medway, the Archbishops Palace, heritage centre and known to some – the prison.

Route Description

1.   From layby go E uphill past Lower Bell, under A229. Cross slip RD up minor RD, past houses and SA on stony BOAT, technical to top. TR on tarmac RD flat to T-junction after 1.5km.

2.   TL, and after 100m TR at T-junction and follow meandering RD parallel to M2 to XRDS. SA and now gentle downhill to Bredhurst. (You can see Southend from this RD!). TR opposite Bredhurst Bell pub, on RD.

3.   Just before church TR on stony BOAT. Downhill then flat to switchback L. Then steep uphill in woods SA to brow and flat. FR and FR again to go downhill then VL up steep stony

hill and flat to RD at 800608.

4. TR on flat, SA past farms, then take first R. Follow RD to go 90L then on for 1km to another 90L. (You can TL here to visit viewpoint at 799587). Go SA here on flat BOAT to scarp of Downs. Before reaching stables, TR on ash BRWAY along Downs in woods to reach gate and RD after 2km.

5. TL, and start to descend hill. After 250m TL on elusive BRWAY and steep, woody downhill, to meet another path. TR and continue downhill on flinty track and VR to reach RD. TR and at T-junction TR (SA) to follow base of Downs. Where RD switches R uphill, go L past chevronboards (SA).

6. SA on tarmac BOAT, and after 500m SA alongside fields on undulating track, eventually downhill. Continue past the White Horse Stone (in the future over the High Speed Rail Link) to fuel station. TR before station on RD under A229 subway on BOAT to T-junction. TL for 50m then TR on BOAT in woods to RD. TR up steep hill back to layby and finish.

Extensions and Diversions
A 7km road ride will link you with Route 8 – Charing 1.

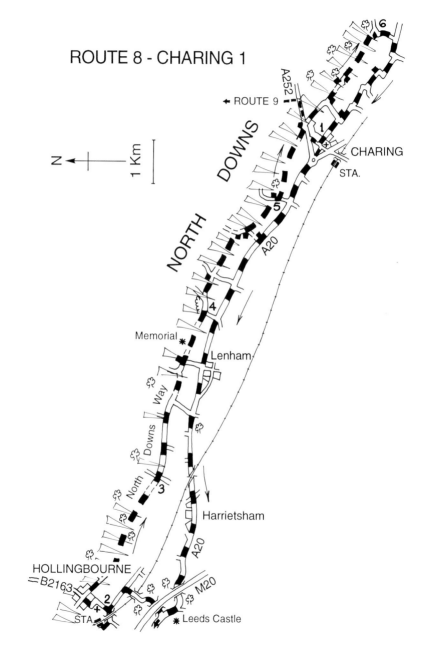

ROUTE 8 - CHARING 1

N

1 Km

NORTH DOWNS

A252

← ROUTE 9

6

1

CHARING STA.

5

A20

4

Memorial

Lenham

North Downs Way

3

Harrietsham

A20

HOLLINGBOURNE

B2163

2

STA.

M20

Leeds Castle

ROUTE 8 – CHARING 1

Introduction

This route fulfils many aims. It may serve as a gentle route for any rider, particularly families wanting to do something a bit longer or perhaps an introductory route for the fit road cyclist just turning to cycling off road, as there are no technical sections on this ride – much of it is grass. It may also be used as a training route for those wishing to have a blast along the A20, a much quieter A-road since the opening of the M20.

For those wanting to reduce the distance, or avoid any A road mileage, then the train can be taken at the beginning of the journey, between Charing and Hollingbourne.

The route follows the North Downs Way along the foot of the Downs, on very gentle terrain. It also coincides with the Pilgrims Way. On top of the Downs is a much older trackway, that would have been followed into France before The Channel was formed. This route can be linked with Route 9 – Charing 2, to provide two very different rides in the same day.

Grade: Moderate
Duration: 3.5hrs
Distance: 37km (without train)
Ascent: 500m
Maps: 188 and 189
Links: Route 9 – Charing 2

Start: Charing at 954495. Plenty of parking in the village.
Alternative starts: Hollingbourne village or rail station.
Refreshments: Several villages on the A20 have shops and pubs, but there are no refreshments on the North Downs Way.
Care: Take care on the A20, and when crossing the narrow lanes on the Downs.

Attractions on route
Leeds Castle: This is often quoted as the 'loveliest castle in the world' and it sits on an island in a 10 acre lake, itself set in 500 acre grounds, with a park crafted by Capability Brown. The park is teeming with wildlife and hosts many exclusive events. The castle was started in stone in 1119. Unfortunately, no bikes are allowed in the grounds, but you can enter on footpaths, as long as you don't stray into the private areas.
White Cross: Large war memorial cross carved into the chalk at 905528.
Gliders: These can often be seen performing above Charing, as they are launched from the gliding club at 978493. You can ascend the BOAT above Burnt House Farm to watch them take off.

Attractions off route
Pluckley: The most haunted village in the country, and filming site for 'The Darling Buds of May'.
Kingswood: Just south of Harrietsham is a 1400 acre wood of hardwood, conifer and chestnut containing many bridleways and deer.
Maidstone: The county town is just a few miles away, and has many places to eat for the hungry rider.

Route Description
1. From Charing, either take the train to Hollingbourne Station or cycle NW along the A20 towards Maidstone. If you choose the latter, then after 11km you pass under the M20 motorway, up a hill then TR into wooded RD. (You could cross A20 here and visit Leeds Castle). Go back under the M20, then uphill, then down through wood over railway to T-junction. TL 600m to T-junction at B2163. If you have taken the train, then at the B2163 TL under railway to this same T-junction. We are now all at the same place at 842548.

2. Uphill on the B2163 past church to XRDS. TR at Dirty Habit pub/restaurant, and follow the Pilgrims Way RD, soon turning to BOAT. Follow this across fields to hedge. VL then R under trees soon uphill then down again to join RD to reach XRDS.

3. SA (CARE) on undulating RD to BOAT again. Follow this to another RD, and TR downhill for 150m. Then TL at BOAT and through gate across fields, past white cross on L, to trees at gate and then to RD at 912525.

4. TL uphill on RD for 400m past quarry on L. Then TR on BOAT down to RD. SA HL to BOAT for over 1km and then down to farm buildings at 932515. Follow track down through farm to TL on BOAT across fields then to follow headland to RD.

5. TR 50m and TL between hedges on BOAT. After 2km reach A252 – Charing Hill. SA on Pilgrims Way, and at 90R TL (SA) to Burnt House Farm. Follow BOAT through the farm in woods along bottom of the Downs – the nicest part of the

Memorial cross above Lenham

route. After 2km TR at the RD.

6. Downhill to T-junction. TR and follow the lanes towards Charing. That is, TR, FR, TR, and SA into the village.

Extensions and Diversions
A 7km road ride will link you with Route 7 – Blue Bell Hill 2. A 5km road ride will get you to Pluckley.

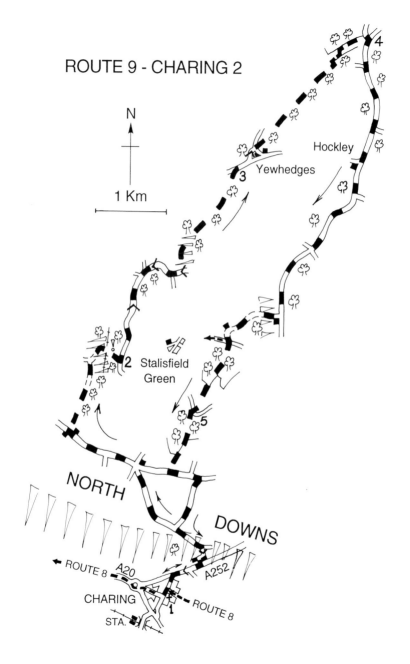

ROUTE 9 - CHARING 2

N

1 Km

Hockley

Yewhedges

3

4

2

Stalisfield
Green

5

NORTH

DOWNS

ROUTE 8

A20

A252

CHARING

ROUTE 8

STA.

1

ROUTE 9 – CHARING 2

Introduction
A route woven into the myriad of dry valleys of the North Downs dip slope. This route should reward the more adventurous group or provide solitude for the individual. You can break away from the main circuit at many points in order to visit Stalisfield Green. This route can be combined with Route 8 – Charing 1, for the more ambitious.

Grade: Moderate
Duration: 3hrs
Distance: 24km
Ascent: 370m
Maps: 178 and 189
Links: Route 8 – Charing 1
Start: Charing at 954495. Plenty of parking in the village.
Alternative starts: Stalisfield Green. Awkward to park, but there is a big pub carpark. Check with the landlord first, you may be obliged to have a pint.
Refreshments: A few remote pubs and Charing has many shops and pubs. Also the A20 has a few garages.
Care: Horse-riders are active in this area.

Attractions on route
Charing: It has a windmill on the hill and some other quaint features.
Private Railway: In the woods at 944528 you will find a railway bridge! I can only imagine that the train took wealthy visitors from Otterden Place to see the view from the Downs.

Attractions off route
Stalisfield Green: An idyllic village green, with a pub on it. Bliss.

Pg. 79: On the North Downs above Charing

Route Description

1. From Charing, ascend Charing Hill heading roughly E on A252 and TL at 960500 up minor RD steeply to top. TL, and follow RD SA to junction. Take RD to Warren Street (L) and BOAT on R at 939518. TR and follow BOAT alongside woods down to T-junction. TR up steep hill over railway bridge in woods to RD.

2. TL, and follow RD N, down steep hill. FR at bottom, beneath Otterden Place, up steep hill. Near brow, at 955539 TL on BRWAY steeply downhill and then levelling out in wooded valley to RD at 962553.

3. TR uphill, soon FL down steep hill to junction. SA on BRWAY along valley floor again in woods and then along wood edge. Cross valley floor to other wood at 976571. Follow wood edge to RD.

4. TR, TR again, and follow RD up valley floor for 4km. Ignore all side turns, to reach BRWAY on R at 969533. Ascend this track past farm to RD. SA RD on BRWAY soon into woods on valley floor. Exit woods at gate and continue across grazing field to gate at RD, 957521.

5. SA RD and continue up BRWAY along valley floor to RD. TL and next R to retrace outward route back to Charing. That is, TL and TR down to Charing Hill.

Extensions and Diversions

As already mentioned, take a detour to visit the pub at Stalisfield Green, 954529.

Hail a horse and dismount

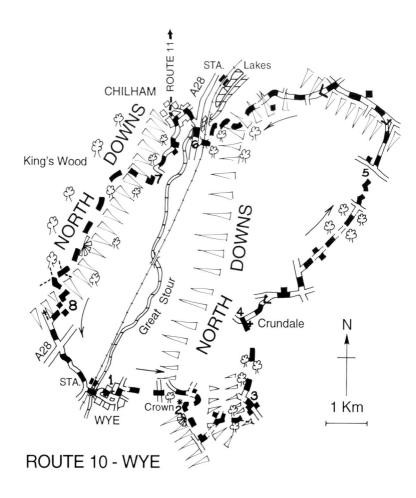

ROUTE 10 - WYE

ROUTE 10 – WYE

Introduction
A major route either side of the Stour valley involving several ascents of the North Downs scarp slope and valley sides in the dip slope. A most rewarding route for any rider. For the complete hammerhead, it can be linked with Route 11 – Chilham, which in turn can be linked to two others!

Grade: Difficult
Duration: 4.5hrs
Distance: 34km
Ascent: 620m
Maps: 179 or 189
Links: Route 11 – Chilham
Start: Wye at 052467. Carpark in the village.
Alternative starts: Chilham, Challock, Chartham, Crundale – yes, everything begins with 'C' around here.
Refreshments: Several pubs and shops on route, especially The Tickled Trout on the Stour at Wye and The Compasses at Sole Street. Wye has a CO-OP and toilets.
Care: An area popular with horse-riders.

Attractions on route
Wye Agricultural College: This is part of the University of London, therefore making Wye the smallest University Town in Britain.

Wye Downs: A nature reserve of downland and woods, containing the prominent chalk crown which was first cut to commemorate the coronation of Edward VII in 1902.
River Stour: This river is crossed twice on this route, and has an extensive area of flooded gravel quarries – nature reserves for much wildfowl. The river rises at Lenham and reaches the sea near Sandwich. The A28 in the Stour valley was the route of the 1994 Le Tour as they left Canterbury.

Attractions off route
Chilham: The charming village square is worth the short diversion up the hill off the route.
King's Wood: A massive FC wood near Challock, with a carpark at 024500. Excellent trails for all abilities.
Ashford: A large market town, known as a major railway junction. The town will rise in profile with the site of the International Terminal for the Channel Tunnel and High Speed Rail Link.

Route Description
1. From Wye carpark TR past church and take next L and then R at BRWAY. Follow uphill to RD. SA, up BRWAY to gate and into wood, and technical climb over roots to RD. TR uphill and FR through gate on BOAT to follow LH edge of field to gates. Through these 90R still following LH edge, through another gate, and LH edge still, to reach a gate on L. Through this and follow RH edge of field to tree on horizon, then through gate ahead at 073465 – massive view. Crown below you.

2. TL along top of scarp slope to gate. HL to gate gap and RD. TL on BOAT downhill to farm. TR just before farm on

BOAT up through gate and HL. Then after 50m TR uphill to gate in wood. Up through wood to fork. FL down track and then uphill past house to RD at 088466.

3. TL downhill on track for 200m. (NB! From Hassell Street to Pett St. Farm are two paths. Only the footpath is marked on the OS, but you must use the old county road, running parallel. You do not have right of way on footpaths). Then FR at BOAT. Up slightly and then along ridge through woodland on gravel track to reach gate after 1km. Through and down RH edge of field to church and gate to carpark and RD.

4. TR and downhill. VL at bottom to go uphill very steeply. TR at top past The Compasses Inn to XRDS. TL 600m and then take BRWAY on R. Through farms on RD then in woods, ignoring side turns. Eventually cross main track into wood on minor path into orchard at 114514. TR and follow RH edge of orchard to RH corner then into wood for 20m. Take 90R and through more orchard to RD at T-junction, 118522.

5. SA past cricket green down into dip and up again. VL at junction and up to wider road. TL along ridge past T-junction to second T-junction. TL and descend ignoring T-junction on L and R, to 90R. SA here on BOAT and RUPP following wood on LH field edge. Ignore turns and eventually TR over railway bridge to A28.

6. TR along RD to just past layby over river then TL over lowlands to T-junction. TL and then L again at the pink Woolpack Inn. Climb steadily uphill and where RD goes 90L go SA through gate to follow North Downs Way, on BOAT.

7. Cycle through woods to end opposite gate. VR uphill steeply to top of Downs. Track bears 90L before gate. Ignore two R turns, and SA on flat to a clearing and viewpoint. Downhill then TR up track to main track junction. SA on small path slightly uphill, ignoring side turns. SA to junction, 30m before gate. TL here following grass path on flat then down. VL to gate (CARE). Through gate and down meandering path to Soakham Farm.

8. SA through farm up to RD. TL here and down to A28. SA HR on RD to railway crossing, river weirs and the Tickled Trout pub. Cross river and TL back to carpark.

Extensions and Diversions
A 4km road ride will link you with Route 15 – Minnis. You may wish to replicate Le Tour, as the 'Peleton' raced up White Hill in 1994 for a hill climb. This route descends the bottom of this hill from 038487. Chilham square is only just off route, and is worth a visit. King's Wood near Challock is a huge area of FC land and is worth exploring.

WYE CHURCH

ROUTE 11 - CHILHAM

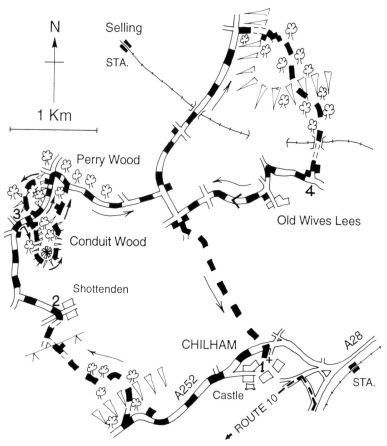

ROUTE 11 – CHILHAM

Introduction

This route combines rolling downland with deep woodland, orchard and one particular area that is a myriad of bridleways – you may just not want to leave it in order to complete the rest of the route. Excellent to take the family out on once they've got a bit more skilled. For the very fit, the route can be linked with Route 10 – Wye.

Grade: Moderate
Duration: 3hrs
Distance: 21km
Ascent: 370m
Maps: 179
Links: Route 10 – Wye
Start: Chilham square at 068536. There is parking just outside the village as the square gets very busy. Chilham is a most delightful place – be prepared to explore, and be patient with all the tourists.
Alternative starts: Perry Wood carpark – also busy. Selling village and rail station would be better.
Refreshments: Plenty in the village of Chilham and some in Selling and Shottenden. Pub at Perry Wood.
Care: Family walkers at Perry Wood so ride slowly.

Attractions on route
Chilham Castle: Chilham would be an attraction even without the castle, so you are spoilt with the addition of this. It hosts many events, especially mediaeval jousting and falconry displays.
Perry Wood: This 150 acre wood has a network of bridleways amongst delightful woodland, and extensive views from the tops of its steep hills.

Attractions off route
Chilham: Down by the river there is a heron colony and a water mill.

Route Description
1. Leave the village square by passing down the side of the church on a BRWAY and descend to the A252. TL, and follow this RD SW and uphill for 2km past Dane Court to BOAT on R. TR steeply uphill on good track to level out under pylons to track. TR to XRDS at Shottenden.

2. SA on RD until junction. TR and then R again uphill to pub at 042552. You are now in the centre of a complex network of BRWAYS. I describe just one loop. Take the BRWAY S past the pub and house following it in woods L around the bottom of the hill soon swinging N and undulating downhill past a house then up to the RD at 045556. TL up to XRDS. TL a few metres, then TR up steep BRWAY soon with earthworks on L, and down steep hill to RD and pub again.

3. TL, back to XRDS. TR downhill 1km to T-junction. TL to XRDS. SA over railway for 1km to T-junction at 064572. TR up steep BRWAY past building to BRWAY on L just before

Approaching the summit of Perry Wood

cottage. TL on into wood. TR and follow flat then long downhill. VL then VR out of wood over railway through Lower Ensden farm to RD.

4. TR uphill to T-junction. TL to top of hill and first buildings of Old Wives Lees. TR downhill to XRDS. SA 300m to Stone Stile Farm. TL through farm on BRWAY then through fields and orchards soon to head towards Chilham Church and A252. Cross RD taking short BRWAY up past the church again to finish at the square.

Extensions and Diversions
A 9km ride down the A28 will get you into the centre of Canterbury. A 3km road ride will link you with Route 12 – Blean 1.

94

ROUTE 12 – BLEAN 1

Introduction
This route aims to introduce the family rider to longer hills and harder paths, and provides extensive views over the Thames Estuary. The eye may stretch to Southend and Foulness Island in Essex, as well as the marshes of the Thames Estuary, Swale and the Isle of Sheppey. The route can be linked to Route 13 – Blean 2, to provide a figure-of-eight route for the more adventurous.

Grade: Moderate
Duration: 2.5hrs
Distance: 19km
Ascent: 290m
Maps: 179
Links: Route 13 – Blean 2

Start: Blean at 122608. Parking can be found in the village.
Alternative starts: Villages of Dunkirk, Dargate or Yorkletts or nature reserve carpark at 122595. Viewpoint at 076599.
Refreshments: Several villages with pubs and shops on route.
Care: The wood at Denstroude is popular with horse-riders.

Attractions on route
Blean Bird Park: Many species at this centre on A290 at 116616.
Views: Extensive views of the marshes from 076599. The marshes around Faversham and Sittingbourne support the brick and gravel trades, grazing for sheep, and land for orchards. These marshes were used by the gunpowder industry due to their remoteness.

Attractions off route
Seaside resorts: Seasalter, Whitstable and Herne Bay have popular promenades and beaches. Prior to their fame as Victorian seaside resorts they were known for their oyster beds.
Faversham: An old town with both a nautical and fruit market history.

Route Description
1. From Blean village go NW on A290 to TL at road to Denstroude. Cycle downhill then up to 90L at 102618. TR here on BRWAY in wood edge. After 300m FR away from wood edge into wood on track, ignoring side turns, to reach field. TR and follow wood then across field down to cottage at RD, 103630.

2. TL and TL again at RD end down steep hill to T-junction. Here TL through Yorkletts to TL on RD to Dargate. TR in Dargate to BRWAY start at 080614 where RD veers right. Go uphill on good surface single track through woods and farm to RD and viewpoint at 076599. SA on BRWAY to RD and church.

3. TL and follow RD through Dunkirk. TL again just before

A2 on track towards Bossenden Farm. TR before farm on BRWAY into woods. TL and follow in wood until behind farm. Upon reaching main track TR and follow downhill to join another track eventually to RD at 097611.

4. TR and follow RD to Denstroude retracing route back to Blean village and finish.

Extensions and Diversions
A 4km road ride from Blean will get you into the centre of Canterbury. A hilly 3km road ride will link you with Route 11 – Chilham. The northern part of this route is only 2km from the sea.

WILD CORN & POPPY

97

Woodland at Denstroude

ROUTE 13 - BLEAN 2

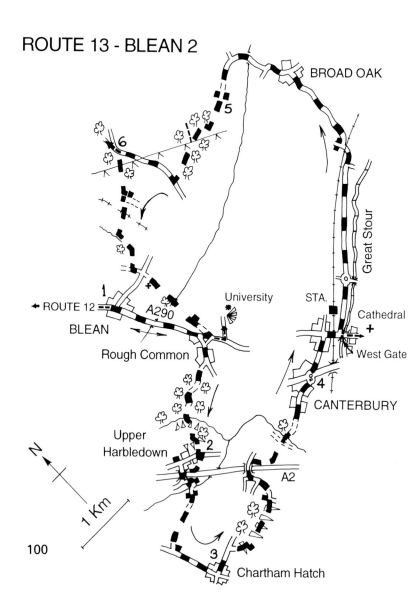

BROAD OAK

Great Stour

6

5

← ROUTE 12

BLEAN

A290

Rough Common

University

STA.

Cathedral

West Gate

4

CANTERBURY

N

1 Km

Upper
Harbledown

2

A2

3

Chartham Hatch

ROUTE 13 – BLEAN 2

Introduction

This route covers a variety of terrain, with woods, orchards and arable land. A road section takes you close to the City of Canterbury. It can be linked with Route 12 – Blean 1, to provide a more ambitious ride.

Sustrans have targeted this area for trails as part of their radiating scheme from Canterbury. Developments could be seen in West Blean Wood and Church Wood and the future upgrading of the dismantled railway line from Whitstable to Canterbury.

Grade: Moderate
Duration: 3hrs
Distance: 28km
Ascent: 400m
Maps: 179
Links: Route 12 – Blean 1
Start: Blean at 122608. Parking can be found in the village.
Alternative starts: Villages of Chartham Hatch, Harbledown, Broad Oak or Tyler Hill, The City of Canterbury or the FC carpark at Clowes Wood 136631. Also, the nature reserve park at 122595.
Refreshments: In the City and the many villages on route.
Care: Being close to the City you are likely to encounter more pedestrians. Some of the roads may be busy.

Attractions on route
Canterbury: Famous for its cathedral and the burial place of Thomas A'Becket in a massive crypt. The City also boasts numerous quaint streets, a museum, a castle and fortified

Pg. 99: In the woods at Rough Common

West Gate, the award winning Canterbury Tales visitor centre, the King's School – the oldest in the country, and an underground Roman museum.

Attractions off route
Clowes Wood: This 580 acre FC wood has good tracks, views and toilets.
Wealden Forest Park/Brambles Forest Park: These areas are popular with families due to the wildlife on display at the zoo farm.
Nature Reserves: Several in the area can be explored on foot.

Route Description
1. From Blean village go SE on A290 towards Canterbury to TR into Rough Common Road. Follow to junction after 400m and FR into Ross Gardens on BRWAY down into woods. Soon VL over stream up steep hill then down steep hill to RD at 116584.

2. TL a few metres to TR on BRWAY up track, soon through orchard and field to edge of A2. TR along field edge to gate and RD. TL over A2, then L again down into Poldhurst Farm. Head R on BRWAY and up through orchards to RD at Denstead Farm.

3. TL to XRDS at Chartham Hatch. TL 800m to BRWAY on R. Follow this fenced path, downhill at first, to track and buildings. SA to RD at 120576. SA 150m, TR at T-junction over A2 again. TR through gate on BRWAY following edge of A2. Ignore first L then VL down through orchard and across stream on track. Then follow fenced path through estate to join Mill Lane to roundabout.

4. Cross and follow London Road to St. Dunstan's Street (A290). TR over railway then TL at North Lane (West Gate ahead). Follow this RD SA roundabout then 4km over railway uphill to Broad Oak. In centre of village at 90R, TL and follow RD downhill, over stream, uphill and VL to Mayton Farm.

5. SA on BRWAY through farm and double gates on double track between hedges to field. TR, on single track, soon 90L into wood alongside fence to junction under pylons. SA and out to RD. TR on RD for 1km under pylons again to take BRWAY on L, before RD forks.

6. Follow BRWAY through wood under pylons and across fields, to VL then 90R across Well Court courtyard. Continue across more fields and dismantled railway for 700m to a small ditch. TL, on BOAT, soon on path in double hedge to join track. You reach RD at 129608. SA on track past church, downhill over stream, then uphill to RD. SA to A290. (University on L). TR downhill then uphill to Blean and finish.

Extensions and Diversions
A 4km ride down the hill to Canterbury or to the university campus with fine views of the City and its cathedral. Clowes Wood at 136631 is an area of FC land just off route, well worth a visit. The northern part of this route is only 6km from the sea.

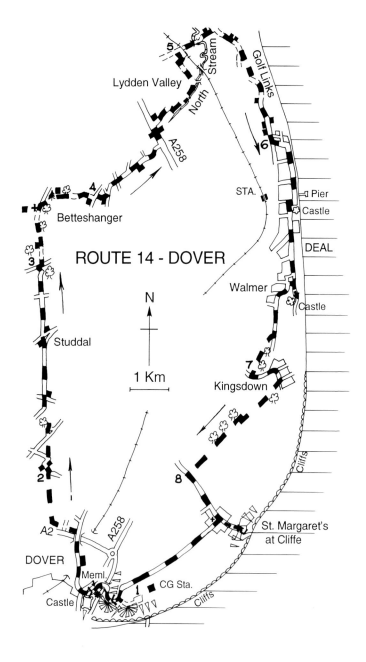

ROUTE 14 - DOVER

Golf Links

5

Lydden Valley

North Stream

A258

6

4

Betteshanger

STA.

Pier

Castle

DEAL

3

N

Walmer

Castle

Studdal

7

1 Km

Kingsdown

2

8

A2   A258

DOVER

Meml.

CG Sta.

Castle   1

St. Margaret's
at Cliffe

Cliffs

Cliffs

ROUTE 14 – DOVER

Introduction
This route passes numerous places of interest and is all the more exciting because of the presence of the sea and cliffs. Although fairly flat, the length and exposure of the route could prove to be a very serious ride for some. Unfortunately, in many places the clifftops are only accessible on footpaths, and therefore not bikes, although Sustrans would like to develop the cliff paths for cycling.

Grade: Difficult
Duration: 5hrs
Distance: 44km
Ascent: 420m
Maps: 179
Links: None
Start: Langdon Cliff carpark, Dover at 334422. Small fee, but excellent views over Dover harbour.
Alternative starts: St Margaret's at Cliffe, Kingsdown, Deal or Sandwich.
Refreshments: Plenty in the towns on the second half of the route.
Care: Can be very windy and exposed, so tog up.

Attractions on route
Langdon Cliffs NT: The White Cliffs of Dover may be best

viewed from a channel ferry. However, you may want to peer over the edge of these famous cliffs from the carpark at the start. Langdon Cliffs is a 7km stretch of NT coast with an abundance of wild flowers in spring and early summer. Nearby is a modern coastguard station. Also from the carpark are excellent views of Dover Castle, Dover Harbour and Shakespeare Cliff.

Bleriot Memorial: Bleriot was first to fly The Channel (and first to cross a sea) in 37 minutes in July 1909. An aircraft-shaped stone marks his landing place, and explains that he was searched by customs and registered as a yacht!

Dover Castle: Known as the key of England, this castle dominates the skyline, and is one of Western Europe's most impressive fortresses. Defences have been active on this hill from the Iron Age to the present. In the grounds there is a Saxon church and a pharos – a lighthouse, the tallest Roman structure in Britain.

Lydden Valley Levels: A vast area drained for crops and grazing. Pumping stations raise water levels. The one passed on the route at 348550 raises the water by about 3m into two huge irrigation streams. (North Stream).

Royal Golf Links: Venue of many prestigious tournaments.

Deal: Cinque Port, and seaside town with the six petal shaped Deal Castle. Deal's pier was the last built, in 1950. Deal was the landing place of Julius Caesar and his army in 55BC.

Walmer Castle: Tudor castle, built in 1539, now the residence of the Lord Warden of the Cinque Ports – the Queen Mother.

Attractions off route

France, Ferries and Hovercraft: Can be seen quite frequently.

Sandwich: This small walled Cinque Port is similar to Rye and Winchelsea. There is a town gate, rope walk on the ramparts and Flemish style 'onion' church. On the outskirts there is the Roman castle and amphitheatre at Richborough.

Goodwin Sands: This impressive sandbank has claimed 50,000 lives in 500 years. When higher up the cliffs you may see waves breaking on it. At low spring tides, the sands host a half-marathon run and a cricket match!

St Margaret's Bay: This place is reminiscent of Devon, being tucked into a small coomb between cliffs. Most Channel swimmers start here.

Dover: Just off route, but is viewed easily from the route. Large and busy docks and harbour serve the busiest waterway in the world – The Channel. You can walk out onto the Prince of Wales pier. The town has a museum, old town gaol and the award winning White Cliffs Experience visitor centre.

Route Description

1. From Langdon Cliffs NT carpark go down RD and up over bypass to A258. TL then quickly TR uphill past Duke of York's Military School then over the A2. TL onto grass BOAT alongside A2. Cross track then on grass again to 90R on BOAT. Downhill between hedges and along field edges through two gates to RD at 315455.

2. TL (SA). VR then just after VL, go R to hedge on BOAT, diagonally across another RD after 300m. Across fields on BOAT to RH edge of wood and along edge to another RD. TR down to XRDS. SA and uphill on RD to Studdal. This is all Roman road. Down over XRDS and another hill, down over more XRDS to beech clearing at 312506.

3. Go to XRDS and TR 50m then TL on BRWAY. SA past farm on L into fields. SA along headland slightly downhill eventually into wood past school and tiny church on L, to RD. Just at start of tarmac go R through iron gate across field diagonally into wood on a BRWAY. Then go through another small gate for 50m to TR before clearing. Stay in wood to yet another small gate. On through trees then follow LH field edge. VR to LH field corner, and uphill on good double track. Soon FL to farm and RD at 322525. TL through double gates 30m to RD.

4. TR 300m to T-junction. TL then FR to XRDS. SA and downhill for 1.5km ignoring side turns to A258 at 343539. TL past café. TR before farm building at Hacklinge. SA on tarmac RD. At end of track go through gate. TR along field edge until you reach a ditch. TL along ditch to pumping station. Past station up onto the L bank of the North Stream. SA, VL, soon over concrete bridge to track, ignoring next bridge on R. SA soon with smaller ditch on L. Track becomes ash to follow through bends to gate, RD and Blue Pigeons farm at 344567.

5. TR on RUPP to cross railway then on double track between hedges through double gate. Cycle diagonally across field following the line of the bent ditch. Swing diagonally again to join track, past Sandwich Bay Bird Observatory to a RD. TR on BOAT amongst the golf courses now. Past toll booth and after 700m of RD, VR and R again. Go SA here on sandy double track across golf course soon between white posts to rejoin the RD. Continue SA on tarmac, past the Chequers Inn, farms and Royal Cinque Ports golf-course clubhouse.

6. TL into Godwyn Road then TR on RD alongside sea wall. RD bends R before Deal castle, so follow RD around castle, or walk past front of castle. Continue SA past RNLI house and two carparks to Walmer Castle. (The White Cliffs start in the distance). Retrace route a few metres back from the castle to turn L on RD from T-junction inland. TL behind castle, up valley floor RD (FL and SA) for 1.5km. Then take RUPP on R up valley floor in wood edge to small gate at RD, 367483.

7. TL uphill for 800m into Kingsdown and 90L. TR then FR here on BRWAY up single track. FR through small wood following LH edge of field eventually to cut back in LH corner to a couple of double tracks. Follow RH track at first. At LH field corner, ignore path on L and VR along field edge then L into wood (Free Down). Some diversion signs may exist on this section. Follow these. Come to a complex junction, after good single track. SA outside wood. Cross another track to appear at junction with rusty gate and continue along the ridge which is much flatter now, to RD at 351457.

8. TL, down and up this RD to St Margaret's at Cliffe. (Diversion from centre of village down to sea and bay is worthwhile). Just past church TR on RD towards Dover for 3km, passing lighthouse and coastguard station on left. Then descend and TL back into carpark and finish.

Extensions and Diversions
St Margaret's Bay is just off route, and although a steep hill, it is a worthwhile diversion. Dover town centre is only 2km from the start point.

Walmer Castle (Dover)

The North stream on Lydden Levels (Dover)

Forest track in West Wood (Minnis)

Delightful cottage near Stelling Minnis (Minnis)

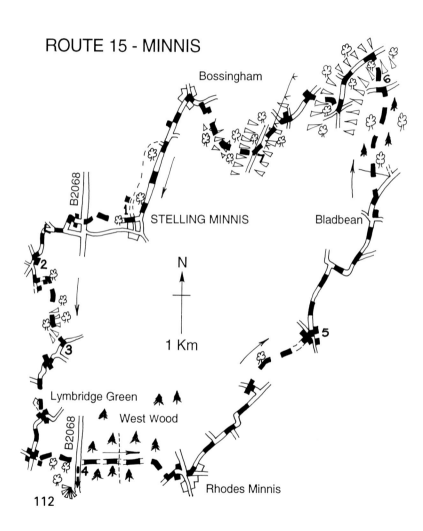

ROUTE 15 - MINNIS

Bossingham

B2068

1

STELLING MINNIS

Bladbean

N

1 Km

2

3

Lymbridge Green

West Wood

B2068

5

4

112

Rhodes Minnis

6

ROUTE 15 – MINNIS

Introduction
This route takes the rider through the quieter dry valleys of the dip slope of the North Downs. An area of much woodland and forest with few distant views – you really can get disorientated in here. The start and finish sections are quite hilly with a very flat section in the middle.

Grade: Moderate
Duration: 3hrs
Distance: 25km
Ascent: 320m
Maps: 179 or 189
Links: None
Start: Stelling Minnis at 142470. Parking available in the lanes of this quiet village.
Alternative starts: Lyminge, FC carpark at West Wood, 142440.
Refreshments: The Star Inn at Bossingham and the Rose and Crown pub and a shop at Stelling Minnis.
Care: Horse-riders are common around Lymbridge Green.

Attractions on route
West Wood: 440 acres of FC conifer forest, providing a carpark at 142440, good trails and toilets.

Attractions off route

B2068: This is the Roman road of Stone Street, and it is worth travelling slightly south to the point where it starts to descend the Downs as there are incredible views to the south and west. On a clear day, the Fairlight Cliffs near Hastings can be seen.

Route Description

1. Go down the R side of the Rose and Crown pub on drive then SA on track onto BRWAY into small wood. At field corner, go R down edge of trees on RH field edge. Then cross fields diagonally L to field corner and diagonally L again, across fields to gap in hedge to T-junction at B2068. SA (CARE) on RD through North Leigh farm, and 90L to T-junction. TR, soon downhill to FL still downhill to reach junction and dead-end RD on L just past Dean Farm.

2. TL uphill then flat to TL across pebbles before cottage. Follow downhill on grass past gate and cottage on R and into wood. 90R on BRWAY in wood then the hedge LH edge of field. Follow uphill back in wood getting steeper to VL then VR to gate and RD. TR to T-junction and TR.

3. Cycle through Maxted Street. At 90R go SA on BRWAY, soon to FL to lane. TL to T-junction at Lymbridge Green. TR, and follow RD uphill to T-junction in Stowting Common. TL on BRWAY down through farms, then climb uphill. Continue through small wood along LH edge of wood. Eventually go into wood at wooden barrier on track to gate at B2068.

4. SA into FC land, on pebble track BRWAY, to XTKS. SA downhill to VR on path. Go through gap in fence between hedges then follow RH field edge out to RD at 147429. TL into Rhodes Minnis and XRDS. SA then first L to follow RD and ignore the first L and R turns. Take the next L, soon to TR through white gate on BOAT at 162444. Follow broken double track, between fences then RH field edge, then LH field edges on gravel track. Continue through fruit orchards, farm buildings and gate to RD at 171452.

5. SA green on RD. TL to follow RD. TR, 90L then FL to staggered XRDS at 182470. SA, then after 200m TL on BRWAY across fields into the wood at gate. SA on main grass track to a bend in a major track. TR then immediately L now on single track avoiding side tracks to a RD.

6. TL, a few metres then TR down BOAT steep to RD. TL, up valley floor on RD. FL to XRDS. TR up steep BRWAY to RD. TL to junction. Take second R just after cottage. Where RD starts downhill TL on BRWAY flat then downhill to clearing. Follow path down LH edge under pylons to gate at RD.

7. TL for a few metres then TR on track and up stony BRWAY into Atchester Wood. At junction at top SA, on double track to XTKS. Continue on single track downhill, to a small gate, and quiet valley field. Cross over to small gate, over wooded rise and down to another small gate. Then cycle up steep grazing field to hedge. SA through double gate and onto track past cottage to RD. TL into Bossingham and here TL. After 1km pass the common to TR back to Stelling Minnis.

Extensions and Diversions
4km and 3km road rides will link you with Route 10 – Wye and Route 17 – Hythe 2 respectively.

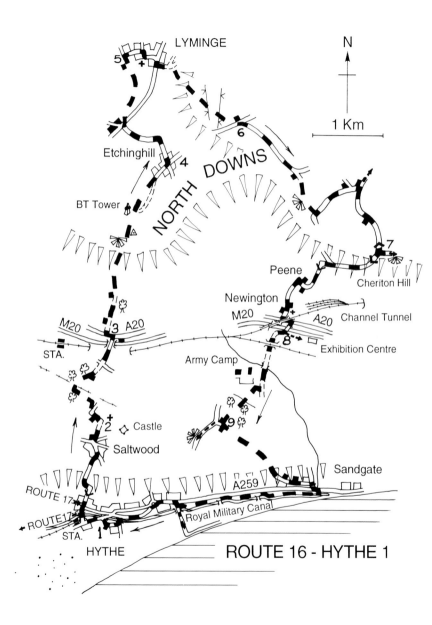

ROUTE 16 - HYTHE 1

ROUTE 16 – HYTHE 1

Introduction

A complex, varied and hilly route that commands many views of both the sea and the North Downs, much of it on military ground.

Grade: Moderate
Duration: 3hrs
Distance: 24km
Ascent: 440m
Maps: 179 or 189
Links: Route 17 – Hythe 2
Start: Hythe. Many carparks available – try Portland Road at 158346.
Alternative starts: Lyminge or Etchinghill villages.
Refreshments: Much in Hythe and the other villages on route. One delight is the Cat and Custard Pot pub at Paddlesworth, slightly off route.
Care: Do not touch any suspicious objects on military ground.

Attractions on route

Saltwood Castle: A little known, but magnificent castle best viewed from the bridleway at 170357.
Military Areas: A large army training area around Beach-borough house has meant the exclusion of the public from

some parts. This has kept much of the flora and fauna intact. This area was where I spent much of my youth as a member of the Army Cadet Force – Royal Engineers.

Folkestone Downs: The area around Cheriton Hill is an SSSI and AONB. This ancient chalk downland was cleared by ancient settlers who walked from Europe along the ancient trackway before The Channel was formed. Nearby is the new A20 double tunnel and an old *motte and bailey* castle earthwork fashioned out of the hill dating from 1140.

Cheriton Hill: Incredible views from here include the sea, the Downs, all of Folkestone, Martello towers and the Channel Tunnel entrance and terminal.

The Channel Tunnel: The entrance to the tunnel is actually here at Folkestone, and not at Dover. It travels beneath Kent for 10km before going under the sea at Shakespeare Cliff, as shown on the Ordnance Survey map. Directly beneath Cheriton Hill is the terminal where passengers and cars board the trains.

There is an Exhibition Centre with a French Café at 187370. One of the smaller tunnelling tools is on display next to the motorway, advertised as 'For Sale – One Careful Owner'! The larger machines are buried under the sea. They did not have a reverse gear!

Sandgate: A major feature of the coastline is the sea defences, with millions of pounds being spent to protect the bombarded shores. The waves over the promenade at Sandgate are quite spectacular in high winds, with the residents having to protect their property with sandbags, and shovel away tons of shingle the next day. Sandgate Castle built in 1540, is one of the Tudor forts and is slowly being consumed by the sea.

Royal Military Canal: Incredible piece of engineering completed in 1804 as part of the defence against Napoleon.

Attractions off route
Paddlesworth: Cat and Custard Pot pub and Paddlesworth church are quite special.
Creteway Road: Route of ancient road where more extensive views are available. Take care when crossing the A260.
Folkestone: Large coastal resort and port. There is a Martello tower at the East Cliff that is open for viewing, and a cycle through town to the Leas Cliff is rewarding.

Route Description
1. From the carpark in town get to the north side of the canal and Military Road. Follow this RD W to the main RD junction across from the railway terminus. TR and R again up the steep Barrack Hill. At top TL. Soon VR and follow RD over the hill and TL to the green at Saltwood. SA into Rectory Lane opposite.

2. Past church on R then VL. Where RD goes 90R go SA up bank on BRWAY. 90R and follow tortuous route of BRWAY up through woods. Take the second 90R over old cutting (the first 90R is a footpath and not a right of way), past house on R then to slip out onto a drive on R. SA here to RD. SA on RD over railway and M20 to A20.

3. TL then after 150m TR on broken tarmac BOAT past cottage and old pumping station on L. Then follow RH field edge, into army training area and through gate. Through another gate, steeply to top with views behind. Over top past triangulation pillar then to R of tower and across British Telecom entrance. Continue down rough track on L to join RD

then to XRDS at Etchinghill.

4.   TL through village for 1km to 90R. VR, and after 50m TL on BRWAY through gate. Cross small field through another gate then up between hedgerows out of gully to follow LH field edge to gate above Lyminge village. VL into gullied path across common down to gate at carpark, village hall and RD.

5.   TR and follow RD past church to T-junction. TR for 100m then TL soon to FR uphill on tarmac. Then FR again soon becoming chalk gully track very steep. Continue between hedgerows out across field beside hedge and RH edge of sheep field. Through gates and under pylons to RD.

6.   TL and FR for 1km to a LH bend. FR here on rough track, (North Downs Way), alongside houses on path through to gate at RD, 188387. (Many views on this section). TL to T-junction. TR 30m (a diversion here, to the Cat and Custard Pot pub at Paddlesworth may be in order). TR again, up, down then steeply up to T-junction. TL 50m to viewpoint at Cheriton Hill.

7.   Retrace route back to the T-junction. SA and down long hill to FL down to Peene. Follow RD through Peene and Newington to A20. TL under rail bridges, and then TR up tarmac BRWAY over motorway. (The Channel Tunnel Exhibition Centre is near here).

8.   TR downhill to VL on black gravel track under railway tunnel to tarmac RD. Continue downhill soon in woods, and then uphill in army training area to camp with parade square and hangars. Reach gate and TR along fence soon to TL

Enjoying the sea view at the end of the day.

through gate. Cross diagonally over field following posts to gate at wood. Through wood and another gate, then another up to Sene Farm on R. (It is worth the diversion here to go up to the RD through the farm and TL a few metres to 170357 to look at the view down to Saltwood Castle).

9. At end of wall, TL on grass following track in gully between white posts across golf course. Eventually follow a bank into gorse, then on single track through gorse down to

RD. SA downhill to T-junction. TR under bridge to reach A259. TL and follow RD to green space on R after 200m. TR on BRWAY and TR to follow track along bottom of canal bank, passing bridges to reach RD at 167347. N.B. – make sure that you find the BRWAY along the bank and not any of the parallel footpaths. The bank can no longer be cycled, so follow RDS back into town and the carpark to finish.

Extensions and Diversions

A 3km road ride links you with Route 15 – Minnis. A 3km road ride gets you to Creteway Road, more views, and Folkestone Warren. A 1.5km diversion gets you to the Cat and Custard Pot pub at Paddlesworth. A short diversion in Hythe will get you to the seafront.

MARTELLO TOWERS AT HYTHE

ROUTE 17 - HYTHE 2

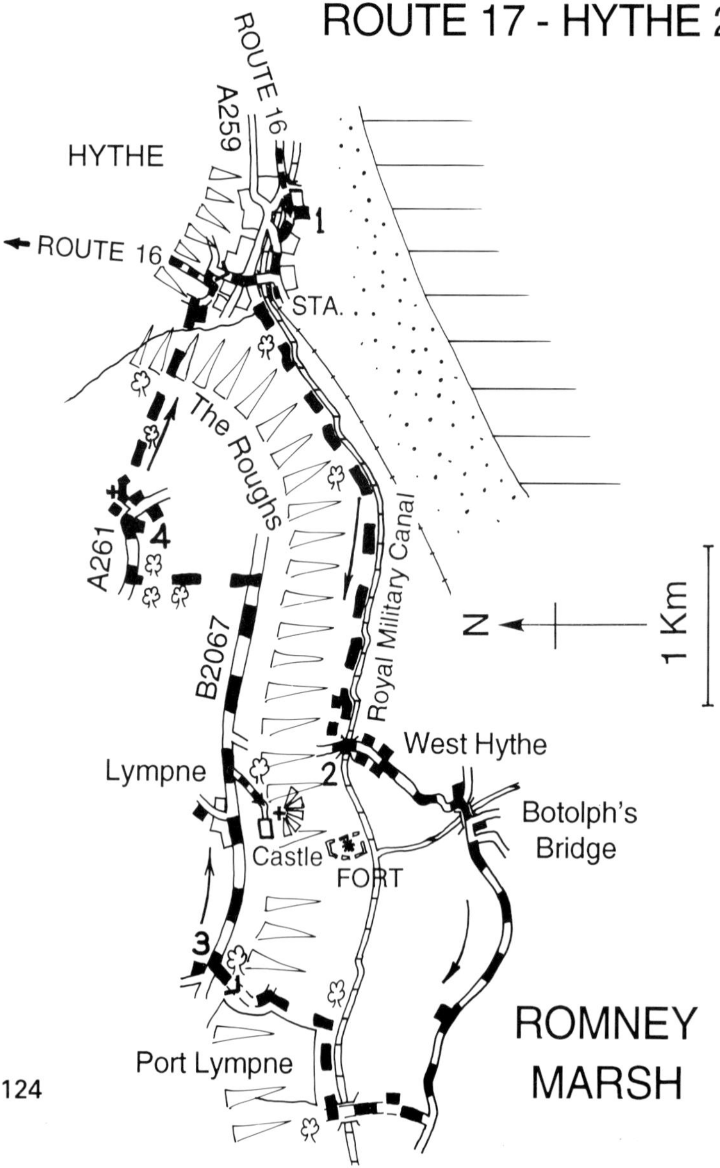

ROUTE 16

A259

HYTHE

← ROUTE 16

1

STA.

The Roughs

A261

4

B2067

Royal Military Canal

N ← 1 Km

Lympne

2

West Hythe

Castle

FORT

Botolph's Bridge

3

Port Lympne

ROMNEY MARSH

124

ROUTE 17 – HYTHE 2

Introduction

A short route on contrasting terrain. The gentle landscape of Romney Marsh and the old sea cliffs of The Roughs provide a fascinating ride past many interesting sites, including the perimeter fence of Port Lympne wildlife sanctuary.

Grade: Moderate
Duration: 2.5hrs
Distance: 17km
Ascent: 190m
Maps: 179 or 189
Links: Route 16 – Hythe 1
Start: Hythe. Many carparks available – try Portland Road at 158346.
Alternative starts: Lympne village.
Refreshments: Hythe, Lympne and a good pub at Botolph's Bridge.
Care: Don't feed the lions.

Attractions on route

Romney, Hythe and Dymchurch Light Railway: A railway that claims to be the smallest public railway in the world. It is 22km long and is one third normal size. Both steam and diesel engines run on it, their whistle being instantly recognisable when out on the marsh.

125

Pg. 123: Lympne Church and lookout above the Roughs

The Royal Military Canal: This feat of engineering was completed in 1804 and was to provide a line of defence against Napoleon's armies. It has an interesting series of 'kinks' along its length. These were designed in order that guns could be trained down sections of the canal on the enemy trying to cross it.

Military Areas: The army have a training area on The Roughs. These old sea cliffs still appear as such at the very top where there is a small vertical face. There are old listening discs on the top which amplify sound – in the world wars, an observer would sit in front of these concrete structures and listen and look for incoming aircraft. The military also have a large tract of shingle beach for their ranges at Hythe.

Port Lympne Wildlife Sanctuary: Founded by John Aspinall, the sanctuary now has wolves, gorillas, monkeys, tigers, lions, and elephants, some of which can be seen and heard from the high perimeter fence alongside which this route passes.

Lympne Castle: A castle and church just off the RD, with extensive views over Romney Marsh.

Attractions off route
Brockhill Park: 54 acres of parkland with a carpark and toilets. The entrance to the park is from the school at 150358.
Lemanis Roman Fort: This was once a sea fort and port, but has since been left stranded. The walls have been stretched down the old sea cliff thus providing fascinating remains to the oscillations of sea and land height.

Route Description
1. From the carpark in town get to the north side of the canal and Military Road. Follow this RD W to the main RD

junction across from the railway terminus. SA down Green Lane. This is the Saxon Shore Way and BRWAY. Tarmac turns to grass track in trees. Continue on this with The Roughs on R and canal bank on L for 3km eventually past greenhouses to RD at West Hythe.

2. TL to Botolph's Bridge and pub. Over bridge and after 200m TR (SA) on minor lane for 2km to track on R at 101337. TR past caravan site over canal bridge. TR on BRWAY along wildlife sanctuary fence for 700m. Then TL steeply uphill still following fence. Join tarmac RD and continue uphill to B2067.

3. TR, past old airfield and entrance to Lympne Castle. Continue for 3km and TL on BOAT down hedged track to gate then through wood to A261. Cross and TR (CARE) and just after RH bend, TL on BRWAY at Pedlinge.

4. Follow drive to small church. TR before church through double gate, follow fence on R. VR to another double gate then SA to small gate at wood corner. SA on single track through wood then down to bottom. VL over wooden bridge uphill on single track to reach a larger track and T-junction. TR then follow LH turns in lane to reach North Road. TR and after 100m, R again down Barrack Hill back to A261 and town.

Extensions and Diversions
Lympne Castle is down a short lane, and a short walk from here provides extensive views. A short diversion from Hythe will get you to the sea front.

ROUTE 18 - HAMSTREET

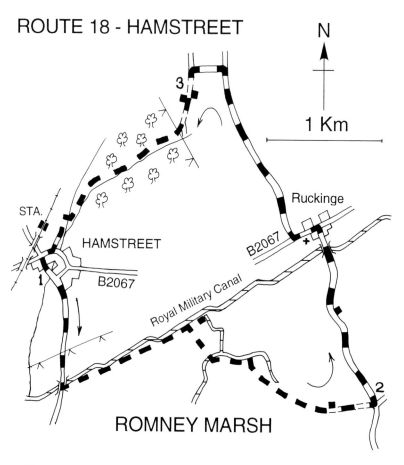

N

1 Km

3

Ruckinge

STA.

HAMSTREET

B2067

B2067

Royal Military Canal

1

2

ROMNEY MARSH

ROUTE 18 – HAMSTREET

Introduction
A short and simple route for the family, reaching out onto the delightful pastures of Romney Marsh.

Grade: Easy
Duration: 2hrs
Distance: 11km
Ascent: 90m
Maps: 189
Links: None
Start: Hamstreet at 003333. Parking available in the village.
Alternative starts: None.
Refreshments: Pubs at Hamstreet and Ruckinge. Shops at Hamstreet.
Care: Mind the traffic on the A2070.

Attractions on route
Royal Military Canal: Incredible piece of engineering completed in 1804 as part of the defence against Napoleon.
Hamstreet Woods: A nature reserve in the remains of an Ice Age oak forest renowned for its moth population.

Attractions off route
Faggs Wood: 350 acres of FC land, with many trails and views of Tenderden.

Route Description
1. From Hamstreet follow the A2070 S under pylons and over the Royal Military Canal. TL straight after the bridge on BOAT along canal bank. Before building TR along LH field edge, over bridge to BOAT junction. TL along ditch, then following field edges to Lords Farm, there joining the track to the RD at 030322.

2. TL and follow the RD for 1.5km back over the canal into Ruckinge and the B2067. TL for 200m then TR on RD uphill for 1.5km to T-junction. TL here then TL at 90R to Gill Farm.

3. Follow track through farm to just before pylons over wood. TR on BRWAY through gate and on R side of stream downhill in woods. Then cross over stream, to park entrance at 003337. Follow lane to B2067 and return to the start.

Extensions and Diversions
From Hamstreet, a bridleway or the A2070 can be taken N to reach Faggs Wood FC 2km away.

The Royal Military Canal on Romney Marsh near Hamstreet

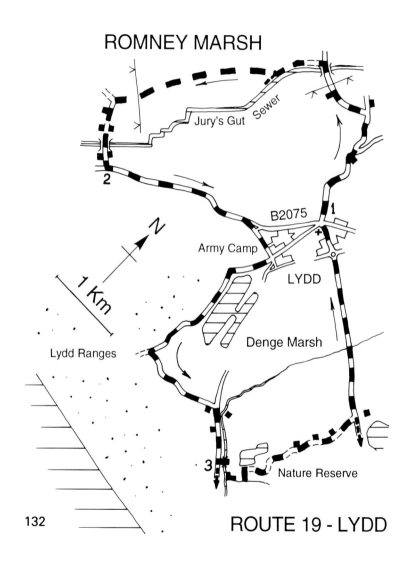

ROMNEY MARSH

Jury's Gut Sewer

2

N

1 Km

B2075

Army Camp

LYDD

Lydd Ranges

Denge Marsh

3

Nature Reserve

ROUTE 19 - LYDD

ROUTE 19 – LYDD

Introduction
A flat and gentle family route on the grass marshes and shingle of Romney Marsh. An area of considerable birdlife and sheep grazing activity. The route passes through remote military and farm land. Although flat, there are no downhills on which to get a rest, so it may be more tiring than you imagine. The village church at Lydd and the nuclear power station at Dungeness can always be seen. The adventurous can create a very remote ride, completely on bridleways, by venturing into East Sussex towards Rye. You might just get to three metres above sea level.

Grade: Easy
Duration: 2hrs
Distance: 18km
Ascent: 20m
Maps: 189
Links: None
Start: Lydd at 043208. Plenty of parking in the village.
Alternative starts: None.
Refreshments: Plenty at Lydd.
Care: The area can be exposed, making things chilly, misty, and invisible – so prepare for some desolation, particularly if you intend to use the bridleways into East Sussex. Also, take care to observe the military notices, as they may be firing – and as they always say, do not touch anything suspicious, as it may explode and kill you. Thanks MOD!

Attractions on route
Romney Marsh: The marsh is one of the most dynamic geographical features in the country. It started to form after long shore drift caused the huge build up of shingle at Dungeness. A massive operation co-ordinated by monks enabled the area between Dungeness and the land to be reclaimed from the sea. The progression of this reclamation is indicated by the haphazard pattern of drainage ditches, hedges and roads. The marsh had a big trade in smuggling as small boats brought their wares inland up the small creeks, particularly when the marsh was cloaked in one of its frequent thick sea mists. Many people are romantically attached to Romney Marsh, and it is easy to see why. The best way to explore the Marsh, is to plot a road route through the small villages, visiting the tiny churches, as there are few bridleways.
Lydd: This unusual large village hosts an annual motorbike festival, numerous raves, and has a large airport nearby. Its church, with a tower 40m high dominates the village and earns it the title of the cathedral of Romney Marsh.
Military Areas: Denge Marsh is the area around Dungeness nuclear power station. It has much birdlife and military activity, with several ranges, railways and nature reserves. The route passes a whole manufactured village used for Northern Ireland training purposes.

Attractions off route
Camber: An area of large and sensitive sand dunes popular with holidaymakers. The village is a busy 'bucket and spade' resort. At low tide the beaches are superb.
Rye: A special town with an intricate network of streets and pathways, on a small hill. Rye was once a Cinque Port, but its

harbour became stranded with the recession of the sea. The Mermaid is a rather old pub, circa 1420.

Dungeness: A community dwarfed by the power station – many of the locals live in reconditioned rail carriages!

Route Description

1. From the church in Lydd take the RD opposite N for 2km, ignoring R turn, to T-junction. TL then under pylons to bridge and BRWAY on L. Uphill! On pebble track, TR at fork on grass path. Go SA under pylons, on grass to concrete RD to R of Scotney Court Farm. TL here on BRWAY through farm to RD.

2. TL, for 2km back towards Lydd, through bends and TR into Tourney Road. Follow this for 1km alongside the army camp. Then TR on concrete RD following perimeter fence for 2km past lakes on L to 90L. Follow RD E to T-junction at 049185. TR for 600m to gate on L over concrete bridge. (SA on RD here, takes you to the sea, close to Dungeness power station).

3. Through gates on BRWAY. TR with ditch on R, then VL to follow small ditch on R to a gate. TL and follow fence on R to a lake. TR through gate on pebble track, meandering through Dungeness nature reserve, past farm buildings to RD. (TR here to visit Dungeness). TL, for 2km, then over roundabout back into Lydd.

Extensions and Diversions

It is worthwhile diverting south along the road at 049185 in order to visit the coast. Sea fishing is popular here, with the added attraction of big ships passing very close in the deep offshore channel. An extension on the bridleways to Camber and Rye is very worthwhile, and proves to be quite an exercise in navigation and sensory deprivation.

ROUTE 20 - OXNEY

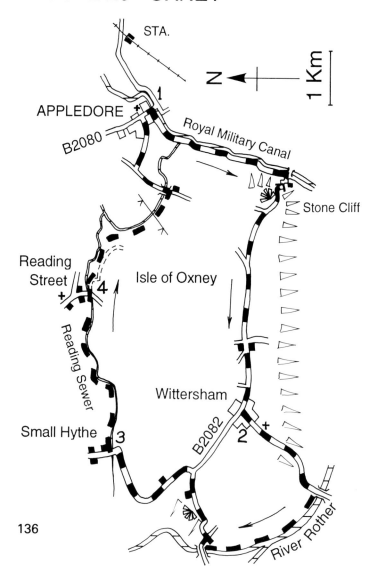

STA.

N ← 1 Km

APPLEDORE +

B2080

Royal Military Canal

Stone Cliff

Reading Street +

4

Isle of Oxney

Reading Sewer

Wittersham

Small Hythe

3

B2082

2 +

River Rother

ROUTE 20 – OXNEY

Introduction
A mixed route of road and pasture, around the Isle of Oxney. The island commands exceptional views of the Romney Marsh, and although inland, has sea cliffs of its own. Some of the paths north of Oxney may be difficult to ride because of ploughing, so this route is best ridden in high summer.

Grade: Moderate
Duration: 3hrs
Distance: 26km
Ascent: 130m
Maps: 189
Links: None
Start: Appledore at 957293. Some parking in the village.
Alternative starts: Wittersham village.
Refreshments: Pubs in Wittersham, Stone in Oxney and at Stone Ferry. Shops and tearooms at Appledore.
Care: Can be a windy exposed area.

Attractions on route
Royal Military Canal: Incredible piece of engineering completed in 1804 as part of the defence against Napoleon.
Old Sea Cliffs: Stone Cliff at 940264 is best seen from the road south of Stone Bridge.
Views: Be sure to look back at the view from the top of the hill

at 940266 and from Potman's Heath at 878282.

River Rother: Full of activity. Herons, swans and fish can all be seen.

Small Hythe: Small Hythe was the site for the Cinque Port of Tenterden. Small Hythe Place is the 16th century house belonging to Dame Ellen Terry of operatic fame and can be visited to see that it has been left exactly as she left it in 1928.

Reading Street: Delightful little community.

Attractions off route

Tenterden: Vineyards and many facilities in this large village with the tall church.

Bodiam Castle: Just inside East Sussex at 785256 – the beauty of this castle is best seen from the air. Built in 1385, set in a moat amongst gardens.

Kent and East Sussex Railway: The first light railway in the country. Steam trains run regularly.

Route Description

1. From Appledore take the B2080 S to the Royal Military Canal. TR just before the canal, and follow RD S for 3km to Stone Bridge. TR, up steep hill and over top to FL. Then TL for a further 1.5km to B2082. SA here to Wittersham.

2. TL past village church down to the River Rother. TR before river on BRWAY along bank, through several gates to RD at Potman's Heath. TR and FL uphill to B2082, then TL down across levels for 2.5km to Small Hythe.

3. Just before Small Hythe Place, turn R on track, soon to follow the LH bank of Reading Sewer. Follow its meandering bank for over 3km to RD at Reading Street.

The River Rother near the Isle of Oxney

4. SA RD and continue on RD between farm buildings and across field to the bank of the sewer again, close to concrete road. Strike off across fields again to larger sewer at 934299. TR along bank, and follow this under pylons to the RD at the Stone Ferry pub. TL here over bridge, then first R after 800m back to Appledore.

Extensions and Diversions
A 4km road ride along the canal/River Rother will take you to Rye.

ROUTE 21 - BEDGEBURY

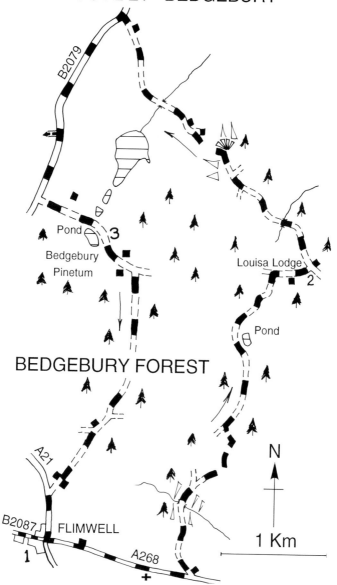

ROUTE 21 – BEDGEBURY

Introduction

This route follows bridleways in and around the very popular 2300 acre Bedgebury Forest, with many of the bridleways coinciding with good quality surfaced tracks, aiming to make it a fine route for all. You should also be able to explore the remaining tracks in the forest, for easier or harder routes. The hillier areas occasionally offer some excellent views of the surrounding countryside. Options exist to link in the nearby attraction of Bewl Water.

Grade: Moderate
Duration: 2.5hrs
Distance: 15km
Ascent: 280m
Maps: 188
Links: None
Start: Flimwell at 714312. Some parking in the village.
Alternative starts: Bedgebury Pinetum. Busy carpark. Fee required.
Refreshments: Available in the village of Flimwell and at Bedgebury Pinetum and Bewl Water.
Care: There are many users in this forest, so watch your speed.

Attractions on route
Bedgebury Pinetum: 100 acres of specimen trees in undulating landscape with streams and a lake. The Pinetum is famous for its world-wide conifer collection. **No bikes are allowed in this area**.

Attractions off route
Bewl Water: Although mostly in East Sussex, this reservoir deserves a mention here. It is the largest area of inland water between London and the South Coast with an area of 770 acres. Most of the 28km perimeter path can be cycled, as it is either permissive or statutory bridleway. However, I would discourage this, as there is much conflict of use. Many families walk here with their children and pushchairs. Horses are also common and the surface has deteriorated, particularly on the narrower sections. During the winter the perimeter path is closed to most users in order for it to regenerate. The reservoir has attracted much bird-life and parts are now accordingly nature reserve. Let us hope that they can resolve the usage issue to enable cyclists good quality access around the perimeter in the future. The reservoir hosts many water sports and events as well as the many land based activities. Other facilities include the visitor centre, café, picnic area, first-aid and bike hire.
Lamberhurst: A nice village with vineyards.
Scotney Castle Gardens: These surround the moated ruins of an atmospheric 14th century castle at 689352.
Cranbrook: A large village with a church called the 'Cathedral of the Weald' as it can be seen from the sea and used for navigation.
Hemsted Forest: An FC area with a carpark in a larch wood at 812343. With over 1000 acres, the forest has one central

bridleway and many forestry tracks.

Route Description
1. From start at Flimwell go E on A268 downhill past church to lane on L. Follow this BRWAY into forest on good, undulating track. Continue up steep climb to flat soon. At fork TR then TL at XTKS on grass. VR then TL uphill to TR at XTKS. Continue on grass path into valley passing pond on R. Go SA ignoring side tracks to reach main track at 735334. TR then TL before Louisa Lodge.

2. Downhill at first then FL over stream then uphill to top and views of Goudhurst. Down through Three Chimneys Farm in Bedgebury Park following main track down then up to reach B2079. TL to reach BRWAY on L after 2km. TL and follow tarmac down into Bedgebury Pinetum with lake, lilies and ducks on R. (No bikes in here). Perhaps have a break here, and make a decision whether or not to visit Bewl.

3. Continue uphill past FC offices on L. At 723336 TR uphill gradually on main track for 2km to buildings and out of forest to A21 at 716315. TL here for Flimwell and the finish.

Extensions and Diversions
A 4km road ride from Bedgebury Pinetum via Kilndown will get you to Bewl Water Visitor Centre at 676338. Alternatively, a 2.5km road ride from Flimwell will get you to Bewl Water's southern perimeter path and bridleway at 700318.

USEFUL ADDRESSES

National Cycling Organisations

The Offroad Cycling Association, Raycomb Lane, Coddington, Ledbury, Herefordshire HR8 1JH. Tel. 01531 633500.

British Mountain Bike Federation (BMBF), Postwood, Kentisbeare, Cullompton, Devon EX15 2BS.

British Cycling Federation (BCF), 36 Rockingham Road, Kettering, Northants NN16 8HG. Tel. 01536 412211.

Cycle Touring Club (CTC), Cotterell House, 69 Meadrow, Godalming, Surrey GU7 3HS. Tel. 01483 417217.

Mountain Biker International (MBI) monthly magazine, United Leisure Magazines, Link House, 9 Dingwall Avenue, Croydon CR9 2TA. Tel. 0181 686 2599.

Mountain Biking UK (MBUK) monthly magazine, Future Publishing Ltd, 30 Monmouth Street, Bath BA1 2BW. Tel. 01225 442244.

MTB Pro. Monthly magazine, address and tel. as MBUK.

Rough Stuff Fellowship, 55 Grafton Road, New Malden, Surrey KT3 3AA.

Sustrans, 35 King Street, Bristol BS1 4DZ.

Motoring Organisations' LARA (land access and recreation association), access guide. The motor recreation development officer, LARA, PO Box 19, Newcastle Upon Tyne NE3 5HW.

Kentish Cycling

BMBF Access officer for the South East – Andy Young. Tel. 01233 634750.

Cyclepathix Mountain Bike Club. Maidstone. Tel. 01634 245398.

Larkfield Cycles, 8 Martin Square, Maidstone, Kent. Tel. 01732 847438.

Penshurst Off Road Club (PORC), Grove Cottage, Grove Road, Penshurst, Kent TN11 8DU. Tel. 01892 870136.

National Organisations

Country Landowners' Association (Kent and Sussex). Simon Ridley, Prospect House, Wittersham, Nr Tenterden, Kent TN30 7ET. Tel. 01797 270744.

National Farmers' Union, South East Regional Centre, Agriculture House, Station Road, Liss GU33 7AR. Tel. 01730 893723.

Countryside Commission, John Dower House, Crescent Place, Cheltenham, Gloucestershire GL50 3RA. Tel. 01242 521381.

Forestry Commission, Design and Recreation Branch, 231 Corstorphine Road, Edinburgh EH12 7AT. Tel. 0131 334 0303.

Ordnance Survey, Ramsey Road, Maybush, Southampton SO9 4D11.

British Horse Society, British Equestrian Centre, Stoneleigh, Kenilworth, Warwickshire CV8 2LR.

British Trust for Conservation Volunteers (BTCV), 36 St Mary's Street, Wallingford, Oxfordshire. OX10 0EU. Tel. 01491 39766.

Youth Hostel Association (YHA), Trevelyan House, 8 St Stephen's Hill, St Albans, Hertfordshire AL1 2DY. Tel. 01727 55215.

The Ramblers' Association, 1/5 Wansworth Road, London SW8 2XX. Tel. 0171 582 6878.

Long Distance Walkers' Association (LDWA), Membership Secretary, Kevin Uzzell, 7 Ford Drive, Yarnfield, Stone, Staffordshire ST15 0RP.

Kentish Organisations

National Trust (for Kent), Scotney Castle, Lamberhurst, Tunbridge Wells, Kent TN3 8JN. Tel. 01892 890651.

KCC Economic Development, Springfield, Maidstone ME14 2LL. Tel. 01622 671411.

Public Rights of Way Unit, Highways and Transportation Department, KCC, Springfield, Maidstone, Kent ME14 2LQ. Tel. 01622 696740.

Network SouthEast Railways: Tel. 01732 770111.

Bewl Water Recreation Office, Southern Water Services Ltd, Bewl Water, Lamberhurst, Kent TN3 8JH. Tel. 01892 890661.